"THE TOWN OF THE FUTURE WILL…"

THE ACADEMY OF REAL ASSETS'
2022 COLLECTION OF SHORT ESSAYS

BY

 STUDENT WINNERS  & INDUSTRY LEADERS

the academy of real assets

CONTENTS

INTRODUCTION

The Academy of Real Assets ("Academy") was established in the summer of 2021. It is made up of member firms from Real estate and Real assets.

Our ambition: introduce UK students, particularly those with no knowledge of the business, to the huge array of opportunities available to them.

Aimed specifically at those who do not have their own contacts, the Academy membership will act as the students' very own "Black book". All members stand ready to help through visits, mentoring, work experience in whatever way they can.

We realise students and teachers are very hard-pressed for time and so, early on, we wanted to launch initiatives, and stage events, that would grab their attention.

One of these is our annual book competition.

Each year, we will invite students, aged 14-18, to write a short essay on a subject that has some relevance to Real Estate and Real Assets. Every student that enters will win a certificate of participation to help differentiate their personal statement or job application.

Each year, the best entries will be published in their very own book.

Published in both digital and hard back formats, the book will be distributed to over 3,000 UK schools, leading employers, universities and the media.

In this, our first year, the topic is "The Town of the Future will…" and the essays will be 800 words long.

To keep our members on their toes, we set the bosses the same test.

And so, welcome to our first Academy book of 50 short essays… 30 by students and 20 by the bosses.

If you are from a school that did not enter this time… please do next year, we would love to get you, your school and students involved.

Stephen Yorke
Founder

ACKNOWLEDGEMENTS

To the following Partners that helped us contact schools and students: Speakers for Schools, The Sutton Trust, Teach First, The Literacy Trust.

Special thank you to Alex Pursey and Jessica O'Regan for their efforts on our behalf.

To Chloe Wong who worked so hard on this and helped make it what it is.

To our Editorial Board for their support and confidence.

To all the amazing Academy members whose enthusiasm, vision and patience has brought us to where we are and whose ambition will ensure that we, together, do some great things.

Finally, to all the students that had a go and entered an essay during what was a very difficult academic year. You should feel incredibly proud of what you have achieved and we hope you feel this book has done you justice.

Stephen

SHORT ESSAYS

BY

 STUDENT
WINNERS

HAFSAH ABDUL

Sutton Community Academy

ETERNITY...

The Town of the Future will be for many but not all, you may not have heard of it but there are a few looking forward to it. You shall know of it even if you are in towers that are built up strong and high. Little did we know that The Town of the Future will be inevitable and will conquer all; young, old, tall, small, strong, weak even king or queen. The Town of the Future will not ask you your status, your value or worth, but your belief and the way you lived. The Town of the Future will endure a journey that's never been experienced before, when heads are raised to the sky and eyes shall roll witnessing something that's never seen before. Never to return! So, here it begins... The Town of the Future is now so near as we head for the six by six. Will it be filled with light or darkness? Will the questioning be easy to pass or difficult with tied lips that can utter no more? The Town of the Future is drawing near. It begins with a blow of a trumpet and a defining blast. The never-ending day is now a start, naked and barefooted, where a man will flee from his brother, and his mother and his father, and his wife and his children. On that day some faces, that day, will be bright – laughing, rejoicing at good news of The Town of the Future being nearby. On that day other faces, that day, will have upon them dust and blackness will cover them as they will not be able to reach The Town of the Future. We will bear witness to bones being recollected, fingertips recreated, hairs turning grey out of fear, smiles as big as the sky for those who will enter the new Town of the Future. Some drowning in their own sweats not able to feel the ground beneath them. Brought forward one by one to be handed the keys to the gates to The Town of the Future. Will it be given in the right hand or the left hand? For those that will be handed in the right what a rejoice it will be, for the gates will be many to choose from. The bridge that awaits them to cross over the final hurdle with His mercy to enter The Town of the Future and enter for eternity. The Town of the Future is finally here, never has the eye or imagination ever witnessed what has been seen. Rivers of milk, honey and wine. Palaces fit for kings and queens made with gold, diamonds and rubies. Total harmony and beauty as far as the eye can see. What happened to those that were handed the keys in the left hand you may be asking, well better look next time... Oh wait there is no next time. A decision made by yourself not wanting to even smell the scent of the new town. Welcome, welcome for those who unlocked the matrix eternal bliss. Welcome to the new Town of the Future, for you understood the true purpose of life.

HAFSAH ABDUL: My inspiration for this writing is my faith (Islam). Growing up, religion played a big part in my life and beliefs, teaching me how temporary and short this life is. I hope my writing allows others to ponder and reflect on the true purpose of their lives.

At SUTTON COMMUNITY ACADEMY we strive to ensure students leave able and qualified to play their full part in an ever-changing world. We are committed to working with our local communities, offering our students the very best opportunities, and encouraging our local economy to thrive with an inspired future workforce.

MAYOKUN AJAYI

Chestnut Grove Academy

The Town of the Future will be a town of revolutionaries, fighting for a common cause. What is this cause you may ask... freedom? Yes. Freedom of social standards, freedom from emotional turmoil, freedom from fear. Indeed, this fight will be for those with courage, standing tall with the truest of hearts. Now we don't mean a physical fight, violence has never brought about any real change. Of course, that is up for debate, but we believe that violence begets violence. Now take a second to think, there has been one too many times you have looked at someone you think you know well and realised you know nothing, nothing about the people you surround yourself with. This is due to a lack of courage, the mundane acceptance of conformity but there is hope. Towns of tomorrow will have fixed this problem. No more people hiding in the shadows of anxiety, no more worrying about the increasing fear of being seen as different to the rest. We know this sounds impossible but this fight for freedom starts with you so open your mind, we dare you. The realisation that you are unique and indifferently the best version of you will indeed change your life. Take a second, unless you're too scared, to think 'Am I the best true version of myself or am I hiding in conformity scared to be me'. Now, if the answer is yes, we congratulate you, you are the building blocks for the towns of the future. But if the answer is no, why? What's the worst that could happen? You get one life on this planet, use it. This is the way of the future, mark our words, we will be those of courage, fighting for freedom each exceptional person at a time so why not start now, be a trend setter. And as for all you naysayers Cesar Pavese once said, "We don't remember the days, we remember the moments." Would you like to be sat old and fragile pondering a life of no memorable moments? Make the choice of courage today and it will change your life, just see for yourself.

Hey! I, **MAYOKUN AJAYI**, enjoy reading, taking trips and listening to music. I am interested in biological research, particularly immunology. Currently, I study Chemistry, Biology and Maths A Levels and aspire to work in the medical field in the future.

Chestnut Grove Academy
"A Creative Learning Community"

CHESTNUT GROVE ACADEMY prides itself on providing a creative learning community by ensuring that students have a rigorous, knowledge rich, transformational education encapsulated through our PROUD values, which prepares our students to succeed at university, thrive in employment and lead fulfilling lives. Our values are also underpinned by the UN Convention of the rights of the child. For this reason, Chestnut Grove is a rights-respecting school in which staff and students actively advocate for the rights of others.

MARYAM
ALAM

St Albans Girls' School

The Town of the Future will be silent. Much like the town of the present and the town of the past; silent in a way that only silence can explain.

In a world of roaring cacophony, silence is but a luxury. At times, it feels as if all eight billion people are standing on the same crowded pavement, shouting and laughing and bustling around. As if the cars on the roads are long-lost family members, beeping and revving in greeting. As if the houses are competing in a rivalry to have the loudest television or the loudest screaming baby. Clamouring school-children pouring into buses the size of buildings or buildings the size of buses. Noisy airplanes stuffed with noisy people, cutting through the air obnoxiously. Even the lampposts buzz and blink when they think no one is watching.

As invigorating as it is, there's never a still moment on this little sphere of life. But say a galactic magnifying glass was to stop right here, right over our earth, right over this hemisphere. It might just discover the small strip of land that is our town. Our still old town enlarged on a piece of glass. Perhaps the sun will be out. Streaming through bay windows and rippling through the trees to make soft shadows. Maybe a short bout of rain will visit. Specking the bay windows and running through the trees to sink into the roots. Or quite possibly, the weather is just still. No sunshine, no clouds, just a town existing in the folds of a suburb. A constant in a sea of changes. A hug to all of its travellers returning from the cacophonous world. A town brimming with memories that echo its comfort. Our town, our home, our silent solace.

My name is **MARYAM ALAM** and I'm 17 years old. I love summer and playing badminton. I also love reading and listening to podcasts. Writing has been my favourite hobby for as long as I can remember. Mostly, I write to figuratively portray concepts. I'm currently studying A Level English alongside Biology and Chemistry.

ST ALBANS GIRLS' SCHOOL (STAGS), is an outstanding all girls secondary school with a co-educational sixth form based in Hertfordshire. Part of ATLAS Multi Academy Trust, we have 1,400 students on roll. We are a Business & Enterprise Academy encouraging innovation and entrepreneurship through all aspects of the core and extended curriculum. Our whole school vision to embrace 'Learning for Life in a Community where All can Excel' is supported by our values of Support, Trust, Ambition, Generosity and Success. Emphasis is on the development of skills for life and future learning.

DOMI ASZTALOS

Futures Institute Banbury

"The Town of the Future will shine like a brand new nail in hardwood!" Said the old homeless man.

Little did the old homeless man know that he would have a big impact in managing one of the biggest businesses in town.

"Agh! I know dad.. I know, I'll make up for it I promise." Muttered the old man.

He quickly snapped out of his visions.

And opened his eyes to the trashed streets around him, the graffiti on the walls of this worn out house in the middle of the city surrounded by gigantic buildings that towered over it.

He swiftly got up from the ground, shaking but holding his ground. "Newspapers! Buy Newspapers here! For only £0.50 a paper!" Came the mutter from across the street.

The old man searches his pockets for any leftover change. "2 pounds! Better than nothing I guess."

He Slowly walks over to the newspaper stand.

The words become clearer and clearer.

"Buy your newspapers, newspapers here!" Says the man at the stand. "Ok! Ok! Stop shouting!" Says the old man quietly.

"Just give me your newspaper, please."

"Alright, fine." replies the man.

The old man walks away, reading the newspaper meanwhile. 'Hiring workers now at Business.co, come to Wall Street now for a chance to be one of the new wonderful employees!'

"This is my opportunity dad, I can do this!" The old man muttered to himself.

"But I can't go to the interview in these old, wet, ripped clothes. I have to get new ones somehow."

A random person on the street hears the old man.

"Hey, what's your name, homeless person?" Asked the man "John, or Johnathan." replied the old man, known as John. "Hey my name is Bill, nice to meet you! I heard you were talking about trying to get new clothes for this job or something" replied the man known as Bill.

"I tell you what, I own a store right around the corner, if you can stand outside and hold a sign telling people to come in, I'll pay you 5 pounds an hour." Says Bill.

"That's a bargain! I'd be happy to help!" says John.

"Great! Come with me!" says Bill.

John the old man works restless hours until he gets paid enough money to buy himself a suit and some normal clothes.

He was usually looked at as a "Slave" kidnapped by Bill because of the way he looked, "Monster, human zombie, sewer rat" were few of the words Poor old John was described as, those words really stuck with him, but it was too late to give up.

"Yes dad, they called me all these horrible names, but it's alright. I'll get through this, I promise, I hope you can hear me up there…" mumbled John under his own breath.

"How long do I have to hold this sign for!? I've been sleeping here for the past three days and I've not even got a single penny."

Bill, the shop owner, appears just at the perfect moment.

"Here's your payment John. £70 it is." Said Bill.

"Wh-What, That is a lot of money, you are really giving me all this?" Confessed Old John.

"Yeah, you deserve it bud, now go find yourself some new clothes!" Smiled Bill.

"Wow, I don't really know what to tell you, thank you so much…" cried Johnathan.

John already sees the wonderful, bright, luxurious shop on the other side of the street.

"I've never been in one of these shops before." John walks in, astonished by all these beautiful clothes he sees nearby.

He picked out a good looking outfit and did not hesitate to go.

John waited in the waiting room. Time passed by really slowly at a sluggish pace, almost like time was going backwards.

Then all of a sudden.

"Next!" Shouts the boss.

John quickly stands up and walks slowly towards the shiny new green door.

He opens the door and enters.

"Welcome!" Says the boss.

"Hello! I am here to apply for a Manager role at your company."

"Alright, So tell me a bit about yourself…" Says the boss. "Well I used to be in the British Army, now I am a retired veteran. I am 65, but fully capable of working. I was a captain in my squadron and I have experience in roles in the management fields."

"Thank you for your service." Replies the boss.

"So what's your adress?"

"I am homeless, Sir, that is why I am here, to try to turn my life around, I hope you understand." Said John, tears in his eyes.

"W-Well.. Uhm…" Stutters the boss.

"Please , Sir." Cried John out loud.

"Well I can't let you go like this, our country's veterans deserve better." Said the boss

"You got the job, you start tomorrow."

DOMI ASZTALOS: I was brought up in Hungary and came to the UK when I was 9. I go to Futures Institute where I study STEM subjects and do employability projects. I would like to be a Game Designer.

FUTURES INSTITUTE BANBURY is a specialist STEM school and part of the Aspirations Academies Trust. Students often come to our school because of their interest in technology and our unique curriculum which has a focus on transdisciplinary learning. In years 9 & 10 we run specific employability projects in different areas including health; environment; design and engineering. These projects aim to develop 21st century skills that will be vital to our students in the workplace such as teamwork and creativity – all the projects also aim to link to employers.

SHARON BENSON

Northfleet School for Girls

The Town of the Future will be sustainable.

According to Google, sustainability means meeting our own needs without compromising the ability of future generations to meet their own needs. This is a very powerful statement that presents a contrast of the unfortunate reality we live in. Owing to the fact that currently, around the globe, we are all suffering from the effects of decisions the previous generation made and the decisions our generation continues to make, this effect is climate change. Climate change refers to the change in the average atmospheric condition in a certain region or globally.

In the UK, we have had a massive increase of temperatures during the summer and rain/flooding during the winter. These bad weather conditions affect everyone in the UK significantly, for example school kids get to school later than usual due to floods, some end up not attending school at all, workers are unable to get to work, while during the summer people suffer from heatstroke which leads to a larger number of deaths each year, the number of deaths caused by heat stroke increased from the average record of 650 in 2018[1] to a record of 2,556 excess death in 2020.[2] Meanwhile, in the last financial year there were 111 deaths, 274 hospitalisations and 422 injuries overall due to flooding.

Should this call for the need of concern? Yes, it should. We shouldn't have to continue to live in fear of what will happen as soon as seasons change, something must be done.

In a survey conducted by the UK Department for Business, Energy, and Industrial Strategy, over 80% of people are concerned or fairly concerned about climate change. This means that many people see the effect climate change causes in our communities and want changes to be made in our ways of living for the sustainability of humanity, amongst the 80% there are parents, grandparents, young adults etc who would like the world to still exist in 30-40 years' time, the continual destruction of the planet stops this from being a reality, it stops young people from dreaming about having families of their

1   www.theguardian.com/society/2018/aug/03/deaths-rose-650-above-average-during-uk-heatwave-with-older-people-most-at-risk

2   www.reuters.com/article/us-climate-change-britain-heatwave-idUSKBN27Z2SY

own in fear of not being alive to achieve this aspiration, it is unfair that it had to get to this point before people decided to care.

One way leaders around the world have decided to tackle climate change to encourage sustainability is COP26. This is referred to as an event in which the UK is working with every nation to reach agreement on how to tackle climate change. World leaders arrived in Scotland on the 1st of November, alongside tens of thousands of negotiators, government representatives, businesses, and citizens for twelve days of talks[1]. This was a wonderful idea and an effective way to get everyone involved, however thinking about the amount of carbon dioxide emitted by the means of transportation of tens of thousands of people makes one hesitate because in the process of trying to improve the environment, they're doing more damage to it. It may be argued that using cars, vans, planes etc to Scotland was inevitable for the attendees and this point is 100% valid, although the numbers of cars used by each person was unnecessary, no one needs 17-20 cars to get them to a conference about climate change, it's contradicting. Besides the extra damage done by the means of transportation, there was also footage of leaders sleeping during the conference, this calls for questioning about their commitment to the decisions they make about the environment, it raises questions like 'did they go there because they care or did they go there to avoid criticism for not being there?'.

Another group, apart from the government, that have tried to influence society's attitude towards climate change is Insulate Britain. It is evident that their protest tactics have heavily angered people, however it got people talking about them and their core message, it allowed room for conversations (in person, over the phone, on social media, on television) about what steps can be taken to support their message while also calling them out for obstructing the road for protesting, stopping many people from getting to their places of work, schools homes etc, which allowed more emissions of carbon dioxide. They've faced extreme criticism and backlash from the public; however many are beginning to see the real meaning behind their message.

A twitter user said 'Humanity is in a lifeboat that is taking on water. Some are trying to bail it out while others are drilling holes in the bottom. And then there are those who are trying to set it on fire!' This statement has so many interpretations, my interpretation is that in this world we have people genuinely trying to make things better for the future, people trying to avoid the problems we are facing while adding to the cause and then we have people who are aware of the problem and doing everything they possible could to make sure it is never resolved. This is the sad reality we live in.

[1]   ukcop26.org/uk-presidency/what-is-a-cop

In the fight against climate change, we all have to come together despite our differences or beliefs because it is a fight for our future and the futures of the generations to come, by not doing anything about it now, we are indirectly saying goodbye to all forms of life on earth.

Is sustainability the future? Yes, I believe it is.

My name is **SHARON BENSON**, I am an aspiring interior architect from Northfleet School for Girls, currently completing the IBCP programme. I have an obsession with creativity, anything to do with art, interior, books, and fashion. My interests for real estate emerged due to the exploration of these indutries and I can't wait to start my journey. During my free time, I run a couple social media accounts relating to fashion which has helped me grow my knowledge about the industry and increased my interest in design, I also go to the gym a couple times a week to keep healthy while entertaining myself with audiobook and telenovelas during my free time.

My ideal day out is a day to a museum or gallery for a new showing, my favourite gallery I've been to is Unit London, due to my interest in arts I was able to get one of my art pieces in an exhibition to take place in May.

NORTHFLEET SCHOOL FOR GIRLS is a vibrant and caring school in which all students can 'Dream big and achieve'. Every student is talented and capable of excelling.

Our vision centres on high expectations for all students. We are an International Baccalaureate World School. We deliver aspirational qualifications as well as developing well rounded, internationally minded, confident learners of the future.

We believe that students can enjoy their journey through school. We place a strong emphasis on creating opportunities for students to lead, take part in trips/clubs and ensuring all members value being a part of an aspirational and respectful community.

AEMUN REHMAN BHATTI

The Heathland School

A SAINT AND SINNER

"The Town of the Future will not inhabit these centenarian ways of life or 'religions'. It will be a modern world, unrestricted by the countless regulations dictated by these 'holy men'. Let us rejoice for the new that is to come, under the leadership of The General. With His command, today we begin the holy war these religions have been waiting for, but the deception lies in that they will not be victorious, rather it will be The Town, their enemy, that will truly celebrate the fruits of our labours with triumph. We will waste no more time. Let us… begin."

The silence woke him. Gracefully, the priest fluttered his eyes open, patting down his regal cassock as he stumbled to his feet. He winced, parting the decorative trims on his cloak, certain that the fatal wound on his thigh would still strike pain in the afterlife. But nothing happened. No ruby streams gushed out, and the deafening whines that terrorised his head before he closed his eyes one last time, were silent. All seemed to be silent here. He turned, somewhat relieved, and studied his surroundings: a simple room shrouded in white encapsulated him, with a solid oak door to his left marked "ENTER." Cautiously, he strolled towards it, tracing his soft fingers over the carved indents. Hesitation flooded in – this didn't seem like what he imagined for the afterlife. But could heaven really rest behind these doors? A sudden euphoria flourished as he broke into a wholesome grin. So, with great strength, he pushed open the door.

Heaven did not lie behind.

Instead, a wild, ambrosial forest adorned every inch of his environment, an ivory kingdom spread far and wide. Vibrant trees welcomed the humble priest and soaring hummingbirds chirped in chorus. A siren carolled in the distance. And in the centre of it all, lay a deep ocean swayed with a melody of its own. Hush … hush … Mesmerised, the priest beamed with such light that the stars surely stared in envy. Yet, in the distance, on a lone island, a grand door dipped in gold shimmered under the ochre sun – a mighty halo ruling the skies. "That must be it". He quickly took off his cloak, ripping away his past life and dashed towards the luring ocean where the sirens sang strongest, yearning for his place in the eternal wonderland he was promised with his Lord. Blissfully, he soared under the surface of the water, a golden hue emerging on the tips of the waves as the sun set. A looming atmosphere blossomed overhead as he swam alone in the soft solitude that resembled the Pacific. Warmth engulfed his soul. Despite the cool wisps of the water caressing his figure, he was at ease, surrounded by miles of the Prussian blue sanctuary. Any memories he had left of his death melted into the waves like a healing ritual. The quaint sunrays slowly faded with the arrival of the dancing stars and the water lulled him towards the banks, a sombre farewell.

Over the pearly rocks he scurried for the door, blinding him in an array of emeralds and topaz. With fateful hope, he pushed with all his might, certain that his efforts would be rewarded on the other side.

The door did not open.

He pushed harder, his hands slipping from the sweat of his desperation. Nothing. And then a voice. Loud, booming. The ground trembled on its command – a deafening aura set in stone. God.

"Mortal. The gates of Hell await your arrival."

Silence. He stood shellshocked and fell to his knees, as if the entire weight of the ocean he swam through was on his shoulders. And behind the foolish priest, the once sacred landscape twisted into a sinister scene.

Powerful winds howled in the east, whipping the clouds into shape. Obsidian armies of rain stamped across the horizon, unleashing a piercing frost onto his terrified body as though some long dead tyrant had returned, armed with a winter fury. The whistles of the hummingbirds fell silent, their wings caged in monstrous vines, and the colossal trees were preying down at him, abhorrent. A pungent odour poisoned the air. Suddenly, the ocean drained leaving a shrivelled land exposed and the sirens cackled as a huge crack appeared, splitting the terrain into two. Shrieks and screams bled into his skull, parasites feeding on his mind. The smell of burning bodies. The land now barren and coarse snarled into a labyrinth and the jewelled door crumbled into a devilish inferno. A mirror rose tyrannically from the ground. He looked at his reflection. A fallen angel stared back. A Saint and a Sinner, the priest took a new name: Lucifer. And with that he fluttered his eyes closed and fell into the pits of Hell.

———————

Hi! I'm AEMUN REHMAN BHATTI and I'm a British Pakistani Muslim woman currently attending The Heathland School. Writing has been a passion of mine since Y6, and I am always fascinated to create a piece that is perhaps a little challenging, to broaden my skills and my personal beliefs.

THE HEATHLAND SCHOOL is a mixed multi-cultural comprehensive secondary school in Hounslow. We pride ourselves on providing our pupils with an enriched and varied curriculum experience inside and outside of the classroom whether that be academic, sport, music, art or drama. We are committed to supporting all of our pupils to achieve excellence in whichever path they choose.

ALEXANDRA SASHA BOLDISA

Sacred Heart College

The Town of the Future will scare anyone, let me tell you why. Strolling back home with Amelia was the best part of my day, the fog obscuring our vision as we listen to the crunch of squalid dead leaves and sticks, cold air like pins and needles numbing our hands and cheeks, wearing warm cosy hats, talking about our day cackling, filling the air with our laughter, cracking jokes and messing about. I looked up at the dark, gloomy clouds as few raindrops were falling from the sky building up more and more. "Should we run home?" "No. It's half an hour away Beth, we can't, use your common sense," Amelia smiled at me blinking rapidly through the rain. I looked around me wiping the raindrops from my glasses and saw a deserted house in the distance over the river, we had no other choice but to try the door. Carefully walking across the unsteady small bridge, we got there, the door was open. But why was it open? Brushing it off we walked in slowly as the door was creaking and stood there in silence for about a minute. "Okay, no one's here we're good," I sighed in relief. As we sat on a dusty old sofa beside the window that was getting slammed with the rain, we both dialled our parents' numbers but no answer. "Great," Amelia commented. "We have no signal here". Panic was crawling up my chest in worry, I nagged "B-but our parents will be concerned, what do we do?!" "Relax, Beth. I'm sure they'll know we went to get some shelter in this horrid weather" Amelia comforted. I rested my head on her shoulder "I'm so tired…" drifting off.

I woke up and Amelia wasn't there. "Amelia" I rose from the sofa, "Amelia are you there?" my voice shaking in fear… Did she just leave me here? How long have I slept for? I search for my phone in my pockets only to find that it was dead, it was still raining outside with howling wind and it seemed to be getting dark. "Okay relax Beth maybe she went somewhere to explore or something. She wouldn't leave me like this." So, I sat back down on the sofa and stared into the darkness in front of me terrified of what might be in it. Suddenly I heard a growling sound coming from a staircase, I immediately started sweating and I felt like I was going to get a heart attack, maybe it was nothing and I'm just paranoid. I'll be fine! "AMELIA, ARE YOU THERE?!"I called out, but nothing. I whispered to myself "What if she's dead? What if someone killed her? What if someone took her? A wild animal? Oh my god…" I sobbed clenching my teeth because my thoughts were filling up with overthinking then suddenly, "SURPRISE! I'm back from the dead! Isn't that exciting?" Amelia teased. I screamed so hard I think it burst my eardrums, "I HATE YOU!" I scolded pushing her, "Why? I'm lovely." She giggled. "Was that really you growling at me? You scared me!" I exclaimed. Amelia had a confused look on her face, "Wait. What growling?"

"Oh, never mind must have been nothing," I replied. "Should we explore this place? It's still pouring outside, so we might as well," Amelia suggested, I nodded agreeing because I was bored out of my mind and my legs were remarkably numb from sitting so much, I needed a small walk. We crept about the creaking wooden house, there wasn't much really, just some old dusty chairs, tables, and cabinets. "Should we try upstairs?" I offered. "Sure, but try to look for a lamp or something because it'll be very dark and we both know that's no good especially right now! "Amelia demanded. We carefully climbed up the stairs and both got very creepy vibes but of course, how would you not have creepy vibes in an abandoned house in the middle of a storm in the future town! "I found a lamp" Amelia said turning it on, "Oh how great we can actually see now," we giggled. "Okay, how about this here room? The door is closed that's new." I said. "Beth, I'm scared" Amelia grabbed onto my blazer holding on to it as I opened the door slowly walking inside and looking around, I walked over to a bed and looked under it "bloody hell Amelia is that a body?" I gasped turning to her confused look, "Beth… what the hell is that behind you."

My name is ALEXANDRA SASHA BOLDISA, and I am 17 years old. I am a student at Sacred Heart College studying A levels. I adore reading and writing, so I thought this book contest would be perfect for me. I'm proud of myself for winning this book competition, and I'm grateful it went well. I am determined, I enjoy taking on difficulties, and I strive to maintain a good attitude, and I hope to have the opportunity to accomplish something similar later in life.

SACRED HEART COLLEGE is an 11-19, all ability, co-educational college in the heart of county Tyrone in Northern Ireland. We pride ourselves on developing the potential of every student by providing a supportive environment which stimulates and encourages our students to be independent and committed learners for life.

We place high priority on the traditional qualities of hard work, discipline and courtesy.

KRISTINA CAROLINO

Chestnut Grove Academy

The Town of the Future will be innovatively admirable. A place where scholars and creativities across fields can shake hands in confirmation of shared glee. The concept of 'golden' paper with a few adoring words such as 'diploma' or 'degree' won't define an individual, and the statistics of numbers won't strangle the necks of an aspiring youth. Dystopian is a place that society has warned through literary means for decades; a paranoia of freedom being lost to masses, and the self-worth of creativity being burned by a blubbering fear that it won't help society.

No. This is a *golden age*, a *new era* of hope and advancement…

As I walk through these halls of where articulate, heroic minds once and still wonder, I can't help but clench my chest at this strange fortifying feeling inside me. I'm lost in thought to this odd tenseness in my chest, questioning if this is a mirage of kalopsia or if I'm being filled with a euphoric exhale of breath. Maybe both. Often I think of the past;

the people who came before me and those who allowed for such a world as mine to exist. It's a given, hardships must always be burdened to one so that another may prosper – if that be in the present or in the future. I admire these people in such a delicate way, I'm thankful they allowed for me to walk these glazing halls with such freshness and pride.

People of the past. Although you'd never be able to physically see how utopic this world has flourished into like farmers harvesting their soils.

You have fulfilled us – you have fulfilled me...

For you were those brave knights that held no title, yet whom wagered their souls upon the very words of books that fathomed their existence, the academically brave who wore eye bags like trophies and rinsed their dying pens upon blank canvases of lines, the voices of a better day shouting through their hearts as if they were microphones. I know you all faced hardships... Your society accepted numbers and words on a paper over your ability and passion, so maybe that flame in your eye dulled. Some of you preserved in black aura of self-doubt... Whilst others were consumed and drowned in its suffocating presence. Doesn't make you less of a great though, because who's to say I and many others of my time, wouldn't have succumbed to similar fates.

Standing firmly in front of the cleanly polished oak door, I inhaled a breath of nerves. The metal plate on the door read, '*Room – 10 where the talented never give up*'. Ambition and hope flared into every muscle and bone in my body like a sudden explosion of fireworks. I clenched my eyes shut for a moment, memories flowing like a soothing lullaby. The type that was lathered in nostalgia. I can faintly hear my mother's honey-laced vocals that awoke me on mornings. These memories held such warmth and orange filters over their vagueness. Because I'm miles away from home, I found myself missing it.

Picturing my father sat at his armchair with a welcoming grin, those deep vocals rang in my head. "You're going to do great things pal. Here's the money we've been saving, so you can chase those dreams of yours", I remember the shock and overwhelming feeling of acceptance I felt, as my father handed me a bulky, brown envelope of belief: belief that my dreams were not just childish fantasies, belief I had what it took to make it on top, and the feeling I was loved no matter what.

My mother was smiling fondly sitting on one of the arms of my father's chair, sipping her lemon tea before chiming in. It's surreal, but I can faintly smell the tangy aroma of her tea filling the room. She warmly looked at me, placing her teacup down.

"Listen, don't go about accomplishing your dreams in hopes of paying us back for this money. Don't take this as pressure or incentive that you owe us any form of success. Find happiness with your dreams, our home will always be here and no matter where you end up.

You'll find your way home".

Their smiling faces and warmly lit eyes are etched into my memory. I exhaled a sigh of relief, and the comforting image of my parents slowly faded from view. Opening the door with a newfound lightness, I was greeted with similar expletory eyes as my own and the same warmth of accepting smiles that I was used to receiving from my parents. My peers waved me over towards their desks, it was as if we all knew we were one side of the same coin.

Thank you, the Town of the past that held the bravest minds.

KRISTINA CAROLINO: I grew up in council estates, still live in one. I've always leaned on the creative side of things; currently trying to make my own music. Honestly, I'm not that interesting, I like the simplicity in doing normal everyday things.

Chestnut Grove Academy
"A Creative Learning Community"

CHESTNUT GROVE ACADEMY prides itself on providing a creative learning community by ensuring that students have a rigorous, knowledge rich, transformational education encapsulated through our PROUD values, which prepares our students to succeed at university, thrive in employment and lead fulfilling lives. Our values are also underpinned by the UN Convention of the rights of the child. For this reason, Chestnut Grove is a rights-respecting school in which staff and students actively advocate for the rights of others.

SZILARD COBAN

John Willmott School

The Town of the Future will be much cleaner than the towns of the world we know today. Many people imagine the future as hyper-technological and hovering cars as the transport of the future. I personally see it a different way. In my opinion, we will slowly but surely work our way towards the use of more eco-friendly methods of transportation, such as the already trending electric cars. However, the idea of flying cars could be introduced shortly as presented by the Klein Vision company in 2021, when they flew with a flying car from Nitra to Bratislava in Slovakia. This new product opens the future for the possibilities of new transportation that until now took hours, may now only take minutes.

Many people these days also focus on the health of people and the planet a lot more, especially after the pandemic as well as both its physical and psychological effects. In an effort to prevent health issues, I think the future town will be a lot more maintained. For example, plants like trees and flowers will be planted a lot more around the towns to clean the air, as well as bring "more colour" into people's lives. As trees and flowers naturally lose leaves and get old, services for cleaning the streets and caring for the vegetation will also grow to maintain the sanitation and keep the beauty of plants. I believe this will be important for future towns as many are unsatisfied with the current conditions of the streets which are littered with trash and also wish to stop climate change.

With the growing population around the world, there will be many changes made around the life of others. For example, the demand for food will give opportunity for structures such as underground or the increasingly popular vertical planting today. This will be used to provide the livestock needed by people around the world, as well as due to the increasing popularity of vegan and vegetarian lifestyles, which means non-animal products will be in great demand. However, it would be blind to assume that all humans would transfer to the non-animal product lifestyle, therefore although dairy and meat industries will still be in business, they will most likely be a lot more ethical towards animals. Furthermore, it's not only the agriculture system that will be affected by the growing population but also the people themselves. Some may claim that it's not only the agriculture system that will be affected by the growing population but also the need for living space. And they're right, however, engineers will not need a new solution for housing more people, as according to Hans Rosling, a Swedish physician, by 2100 the world population will peak at 11 billion. This means that although new houses and skyscrapers will be built, there will be no drastic need for new types of housing, rather than just the expansion of cities and towns to larger scales, which is allowed by the growing vertical planting.

There are many different ideas and thoughts on what the future town will be like, and many have a more optimistic and daring imagination on its structure and architecture, but I think it will not be so different to the changes we see happening today, as the transition to more healthy lifestyles of people, the fight for the planet as well as developing technology, which will change our towns to cleaner and safer areas.

My name is **SZILARD COBAN**, I am 16 years old, and I go to John Willmott School. As I am in year 12, I try to complete as many as possible opportunities that come my way to be more successful in the future in both education and adult life. I would like to inspire and push people to work hard as well as pursue their goals, and especially not to throw away the opportunities that they get, they can be very fun and beneficial in the long run!

JOHN WILLMOTT SCHOOL is an 11-18 co-educational school in Sutton Coldfield, West Midlands with over 1,000 students. The school is founded on the motto 'Potential into Reality', and we instil this into our students' daily lives. Our Sixth Form is small and friendly and offers strong courses that help students go onto study at university; we are a caring and nurturing Sixth Form with outstanding academic examination results.

PATRISHA COLACO

St Mark's Catholic School

The Town of the Future will be a devil's daunting den. The sky is going to look like a land of haunted, spooky spirits creeping up on every individual. Large pillows of threatening tar black clouds will form, slowly blotting out the old gold colour of the sun.

The voluminous rain will grab the necks of many, slowly choking them.

Hissing and sissing like a venomous snake as it'll purr with enormous energy, destroying the soft soil with its wild and indiscriminate plump missiles, splattering powerfully onto the ground. It's icy, the stinging nails of the rain will strip the skin and shrink everyone's soul. Biting their cold nails as their bodies drown in fear and nervousness, or perhaps simply from the deadly rain-water and the melting ice caps. It'll be almost so unrealistic and overwhelming that no nightmare of any human could ever beat. Boom, clash may whip the bright, gloomy lightning with thunder-glassy clinking of champagne flute, crashing and cracking so loud over your head that your eardrums will begin to bleed. In the light of this the non-stop rumbling and grumbling will annoy and scare beings to death as if it was part of a great master plan of the devil as the lightning and thunder will rage in fury. The blustery, brisk, brutal wind, probably sighing and thrashing as though a werewolf had a knife stabbed in his throat on the night of the full moon. In the distance they'll see the remnants of a dead forest, the dark trees lining the horizon like foot soldiers ready for battle. In addition their shadows should look like skeletons, dead and bare. Trunks, gnarled and twisted with interlacing roots protruding from the soil in great loops and ridges. Sprawling branches with no leaves will look like crooked limbs which will seem like it lost its battle against the Violent Wind. Its woody incense from centuries of snapping branches crashing to the forest floor, rotting silently. The composting, organic smell will rise up in waves like a miasma. Moreover, the winds' strong force can strip the trees alive, pulling and tormenting the delicate leaves as they fly away in terror. Coils of vaporous mist will wrap the shaggy heads of the trees. Withering, around them like a conjuror milky smoke, sensuous and illusory. Sieves of mist will caress the lichen-encrusted bark guardian of the town's forest. Furthermore, adding its phantasmal gas to the damp breath of the forest, gliding with deadly intent. Nevertheless, accompanied by air pollution your lungs will feel as if there were tiny chain-saws inside. Its deadened sound, haunting glades will pour into empty spaces. A sepulchral silence may hang over. No one will see the pretty things in the stores of the town for what they were, but for ecological disaster that shall be in the store for all of us if we don't stop this consumeristic gutting of our mother planet. Nothing will stir, nothing will ever shine, nothing will ever sing. The place that once everyone loved will turn into a daylight turmoil.

Congratulations and get ready to see your own future town collapse... you all did it.

I am **PATRISHA COLACO** and I am 16 years old, currently doing my A Levels at St. Mark's. I wrote this short essay, keeping in mind the severe consequences of Global Warming if we don't change our actions. We all have limited time and at the end of the day it is us who are responsible for our planet.

AMALIA COTOVAN

King Ecgbert School

WE DON'T BUILD PYRAMIDS ANYMORE

"The Town of the Future will be built by aliens!"
Silly child, we *are* the aliens. They said the ancient pyramids
Would have taken a thousand lifetimes to complete
By the hand of man. Well, I say!
I finished my own just the other week.
Took a month, bit of elbow grease, but there it is.
Right in my backyard where it'll stay and stay.
"And no aliens in sight?" Now you've got it!
But we don't build pyramids anymore,
We don't slay giants anymore,
We don't love and hate and live and kill like before.
If aliens came to give us a hand, we'd kill them too,
No matter how well they can put one brick on top of another.
"So we'll build the town ourselves." You think that? Do you?
Silly child. Of course not. The town will build itself.
In its due time, one falling leaf will stack and stack
And hope the wind in its ever-giving grace won't blow the stack over.
Hammer and nail it will build itself, and it will take a weekend,

And we won't even see it coming.
"I'll believe it when I see it."
Good boy, the aliens would be proud, if they weren't bleeding
out on the floor. Here come the fairies to help them,
aim your slingshot this much higher. That's a lad!
You'll be a soldier yet when I'm through with you.

———————————

AMALIA COTOVAN is an exceptional student who takes a very active part within our school community. Amalia is always looking out for opportunities to develop herself and those around her. Since coming to sixth form we have seen Amalia develop from strength to strength. She has high aspirations for the future to study at one of the top universities in the country and her work ethic and grades would show that she is destined for this journey. We are proud of everything she does in school and how she supports our school community including younger students.

KING ECGBERT SCHOOL is a large 11-18 secondary school of roughly 1,450 students, including a sixth form of around 380 students. Our school is situated in Dore in the south-west of Sheffield, close to the Peak District. We serve a vibrant and diverse catchment, stretching from the very edge of the city to the very centre, following the Abbeydale corridor; we are a truly comprehensive school.

A 'System Leading School', and part of Mercia Learning Trust, King Ecgbert School is rated as 'Outstanding' by Ofsted, was awarded World Class School status in 2018 and was voted World Class School of the Year in 2019. King Ecgbert School works with Notre Dame School as a DfE appointed EdTech Demonstrator collaboration, EdTechSheff.

VIOLET-MAY DAVEY

Harris Academy Battersea

T he Town of the Future will never be the same again. As the Town becomes more populated; the place becomes different. As the seasons switched from Spring, to Summer, to Autumn, and to Winter; the world changed every time. It was a mystery to the majority to whom was the cause of this extraordinary change. All was revealed in just one day.

When the shining sun went to sleep and the luminous moon took its place, the world was consumed in a darkness that surrounded the globe. All was asleep; apart from one. This was a seven-year-old girl named *Krystal Eclipse*. She had skin as white as snow and eyes as blue as the mysterious sea (with a tint of gold surrounding the orb). Her hair was waist length and black like coal with highlights a bright shade of white. All wondered as to why her hair was so long and why it was unnatural but no one could answer. *Krystal* was awake because she could not sleep; she hated the silence. She always wondered 'Why the world had to sleep as soon as the moon came out? Why the world had to be awake as soon as the sun arrived? Why everyone in town followed that same boring system instead of being free?' These thoughts always seemed to occupy her mind, to shield her from the deafening silence that caused her dread. When it was time to wake up, she was already awake. The people in town never questioned her as although there were noticeable dark circles, her unusual eyes always remained prominent and bold. As if to distract everyone from her true features.

As time went on, the Town hoped for a better future, a place where something different and new happened. *Krystal* aged as well, at the age of ten, her eyes began to GLOW, creating a beautiful aura of a peaceful time at the beach. Her hair (still jet black and white) was now knee length. She never cut it nor put it up. It always remained straight and down. You may be wondering, why does she not ask her parents to cut it? Well, she has none and she likes her hair long. *Krystal* was an orphan who wandered around Town alone and no one approached her because of her strange looks. She liked it that way. *Krystal* patiently waited for the day to turn into night as this was where her eyes glowed more. She lived in the secluded area of Town (a corner where no one would go because of her) but she too yearned for a change to happen. When it was time for night, she decided that she would be the one to initiate that change; tomorrow. She then decided to try closing her eyes for the first time in her years of existence; only to realise that the bright glow unpermitted her to. It seems that she could only blink her eyes but not close them for a long time. This meant one thing; she did not need to sleep. What was her purpose here, was she really human?

As the next day approached, *Krystal* ventured towards the highest set of mountains in the centre of Town. She walked cautiously past every person. She did not want anyone to notice her unexpected arrival so she continued forward; as if she was never there. The town kept to their daily routines whilst she crept past like a shadow. *Krystal* managed to enter the centre of Town as it was not guarded. All that was there was a rusty copper gate, signifying its age. She pressed one of her palms delicately on the handle and with only the sound of a creak; the gate opened. 'That was easy', she thought as she began to walk along the greyish pavestone that was covered in green splotches. As she was walking, she missed that everything around her was frozen and the withering sign at the entrance that stated: "FROZEN TIME PERIOD".

It was turning to night as the glow of the sun began to sink and the moon began to rise. Although everything was still, *Krystal* and the sun and moon were the only things

moving. She approached the peak of the mountains so that she could get a closer look. It never occurred to her how she knew where to go, it was as if the sun and moon called her. Suddenly, her eyes glowed and created a beam of light which stopped both orbs moving. The sun and moon then merged; forming an eclipse. This astronomical event caused the town and globe to alternate night and day. The Town of the Future will never be the same again; all thanks to a girl named *Krystal Eclipse*.

———

VIOLET-MAY DAVEY: I am a very independent person who always follows my instincts. I enjoy reading a variety of books and writing stories. I also like to draw in my spare time as it allows me to use my imagination creatively. Finally, I am hard-working and love to learn new things.

HARRIS ACADEMY BATTERSEA is an Ofsted-rated 'Outstanding' co-educational secondary school in the heart of London. Our vision is to 'develop aspirational young people who thrive in a changing world', which we instil through our core values of knowledge, integrity and resilience.

SAMANTHA FARNSWORTH

St Albans Girls' School

RECORDS OF A SURVIVOR

The Town of the Future will... The Town of the Future will... well I don't really know what The Town of the Future will be like, or even if there will be a future. At least one worth living in. What I do know is that if The Town of the Future is like the town of my past, we would be better off letting climate change get the best of us.

People still talk about that night. The night the clouds rolled in. Some people say that it was just a freak weather accident and move on. Some people claim it was UFOs or the government coming to steal our secrets. Some say it was the paranormal. People wonder what happened, but none of them saw what I saw. None of them know what I know. For I was there when the rest of the town wasn't; when the — the Things came crawling out of the mist and the dark cracks in reality.

I felt the wrong the first time I saw Them, oozing out of folds of darkness and flaps of nothing. It was the mist that created these pockets. At least that's what I assume. It would roll along, menacing in its silent and bleak path, slow and steady across our town. Everything it touched was changed for the worse; Hal's grocer went bankrupt 2 weeks later, Johnny's house burned down the next day, and forever afterwards on dark nights, there was a presence in the town that made people lock themselves in their houses and close the shutters.

It's hard to describe the Things in a way you, reader, will understand. They look like shadows made solid and fears personified. They smell like secrets. And Their sound? Well that's the worst part. They have no sound. Silence follows Them around like a thick blanket, smothering everything it touches. You wouldn't hear them if they came for you; just like no one would hear you when you screamed.

Their domain is much like them; black, silent, and utterly terrifying. It is the sky on the blackest of nights when no moon shines and no stars twinkle. The time I spent there I will never forget. The days bleed into months and years. Time passes differently there, if it passes at all, and one would find it immensely difficult to keep track of it. Out of everything though, darkness is what I remember most. Darkness and cold. Absolute bone-aching, blood-chilling cold. I'd never felt anything like it before and I never have since. But then that's the thing with Them, every aspect of every thing is just wrong. You can feel it, like something rooted deep inside you is twisting out of shape.

Now, reader, you may wonder who I am or why I am writing. I will not tell you my name nor where I am but you may know this: everything recorded here is completely factual. I spent many years after I returned running away from my past, hoping I could forget. But we cannot forget the experiences that shape us. So I returned, and I have remained here for long enough that it is as though I never left. I am worn out in age now and have no kith or kin to remember me so I write this book in the hopes that after I am gone, I will not be forgotten. Here then, is my story.

SAMANTHA FARNSWORTH: I am 16 and have been an avid reader for as long as I can remember. I naturally turned to writing and have spent the last two years practising and cultivating my abilities. Some day I hope to be a published author and have my works read worldwide!

ST ALBANS GIRLS' SCHOOL (STAGS), is an outstanding all girls secondary school with a co-educational sixth form based in Hertfordshire. Part of ATLAS Multi Academy Trust, we have 1,400 students on roll. We are a Business & Enterprise Academy encouraging innovation and entrepreneurship through all aspects of the core and extended curriculum. Our whole school vision to embrace 'Learning for Life in a Community where All can Excel' is supported by our values of Support, Trust, Ambition, Generosity and Success. Emphasis is on the development of skills for life and future learning.

TARA GILLIES

Halcyon London International

The Town of the Future will….
The Town of the Future will be.
Or it will not.

Future isn't singular. There are many futures. Many paths. Many challenges to overcome.

Each decision leads to a different future, so will your decision allow The Town of the Future to be, or will it not?

There are different possibilities. Good and bad, positive and negative. Here's the negatives.

The Town of the Future will not be home to the sapphire sparkling waters that foster our every need.

The Town of the Future will not be home to clean, soft air.

The Town of the Future will not be home to friendship.

The Town of the Future will not be home to self-love.

The Town of the Future will not be home.

The Town of the Future will not be.

The Town of the Future will not be free from the consequences of the misconceptions made by our "leaders".

The Town of the Future will not be free from the undying wails of those whose stomachs are empty.

The Town of the Future will not be free from our constant wars of child-like play. The Town of the Future will not be free.

The Town of the Future will not be.

But then there's the positive possibilities.

The Town of the Future will be there to nurture every tree, every particle of air, every particle of water, and every particle of love.

The Town of the Future will be there to nurture every beings' talent, skill, and soul. The Town of the Future will be there to nurture.

The Town of the Future will be there.

The Town of the Future will be.

The Town of the Future will be free from the lack of respect for each other and our wonderful earth.

The Town of the Future will be free from illness, plague, chaos, and insanity. The Town of the Future will be free from misleading patriarchy. The Town of the Future will be free.

The Town of the Future will be.

Now, how do we turn our future from the negatives to the positives? Let me tell you how.

First of all, our relationship with this earth is not congruent and aligned. Our relationship with each other is not congruent and aligned either. But most important of all, our relationship with ourselves is neither congruent nor aligned.

How do I be in harmony with the earth and nature?

You need to be mindful. Simply mindful. We need to take what we need, and nothing more.

You need to inscribe the mentality in yourself that you will leave the earth better than you found it.

How do I be in harmony with others?

You need to be collaborative. When you feel the urge to disagree with someone else, you need to think twice. What is it that they are trying to say? What is it that they are trying to convey? How do I look at this in their shoes. If we all do this, maybe we will all realise that there is at least one thing that we all agree on.

How do I be in harmony with myself?

You need to believe. You need to believe that your psyche knows what to do, and that you are doing what is right, and in your and others best interests. But most of all, to truly be in harmony with yourself, you have to do the above.

Then, whoever we are, and whatever future we end up in, and whichever town we live in, we will thrive with the earth, with each other, and most importantly:

Ourselves.

TARA GILLIES (Year 12) is a multinational born to Indian Mum and South African, Scottish, and English Dad. She lives in a unique boathouse in Little Venice with her parents and her dog. She currently studies at Halcyon London International School, and will start boarding at the Kings School Canterbury from September, which she is very excited about. Her passion is singing, dancing, acting, and of course, novel writing – especially dystopian.

HALCYON
LONDON INTERNATIONAL SCHOOL

HALCYON LONDON INTERNATIONAL is situated in Marylebone, London, Halcyon is an International Baccalaureate (IB) school that is leading the way forward in education. We inspire students to embrace an unparalleled capability and lifelong passion for learning.

ABIGAIL GOMES

Trinity Catholic High School

ESCAPE FROM AI

" The Town of the Future will be break taking,
Which will be a utopia, which means no hating,
It is said to be an everlasting piece of art,
Technology which means no one should be apart"

As I look at that article from 2005,
I try to see what the author was trying to contrive,
In 2099, these words DO NOT EXIST,
I see in my mind, the dates and disasters they have missed,

As 1 and 0s starts appearing on my screen,
It appears, ambushing me in my dream,
Putting me in a corner, there is nowhere to run,
Brainwashing me, thinking that Ai has won,

The electric signals are messing with my brain,
All these dates and events can't remain,
It speaks, "Big brother is watching you,"
All these unnatural memories coming through,

――――――――――

My name is **ABIGAIL GOMES**, I'm 17 years old and I live in London. I study at Trinity Catholic High School, Woodford. For my A-levels, I have taken business, computer science and photography. When I finish my A-Levels, I want to continue my studies in Business.

Founded in 1976, TRINITY CATHOLIC HIGH SCHOOL in Woodford Green is one of the most distinguished Catholic schools in the country. It is an 11-18 mixed school and Sixth Form. In partnership with parents, Trinity aims through a Christ-centred curriculum, to develop young men and women of faith, good character, strong intellect and generous spirit, able to move confidently into the world and to use their talents and gifts to lead and serve others.

LILY HARRISON

Newfriars College

You asked what 'The Town of the Future' will be. What do you see? Will it be a better environment for you and me?

I am a time traveller, you see. You may look at me and say, "You're just like me." Maybe so, but there's a wide assortment of ideas that only my eyes can see. Scenarios that only my ears can hear. Adventures that only my imagination can take me.

Come, why don't you? I can take you forward, at least 50 years from now, to see what will become of that same silly little town. You'll be surprised to discover so much about your future in so little time …

Now, now, one question at a time. I am aware that many like you have many things to ask about your future. I am often asked about flying cars and robots ruling supreme. Surely there is much more to that than these – I mean, what do you think will happen to the animals? Will there be more or less? Which species will be endangered and which species will come to our land? Will slaughterhouses shut down? Will the food we eat be made entirely out of friendly meat? This, I cannot say, but it is something for you to think about.

The government and its own future, I hear you worry, what about it? Well, we can only hope that in 50 years time that the country shall be run by someone with not just common sense, but someone who will absolutely go out of their way to make sure that everything is running like clockwork. Someone who cares about everyone; those of colour, those with less money or privileges, those who will love unconditionally, those who desperately need that extra support. Someone with a massive passion for helping others, reaching out for others and respecting others. Could you be that someone? This, I cannot say, but it is something for you to think about.

Oh, you are asking me about the technology of the future? It is clear to imagine that it will be more advanced in the coming years, but in what way? We've already welcomed back flip-phones for a whole new generation, as well as other revamped products. Will we continue this in the future? A lot of people are mixed about this idea, as some would rather have the original items than the newly built. Are there designers like you, perhaps, who could recreate classic products with a realistic feel as if it were the real deal? This, I cannot say, but it is something for you to think about.

What do you think about social media? Hmm … Oh dear, yes, I see. Yes, I understand you and other young people of your age find it extremely overwhelming. I am obviously aware of how many taboos that were once slaughtered in media are more accepted and normalised today, but those same hate crimes are almost simultaneously rising higher than ever. Is there anything we can do to prevent this? Is there a way we can permanently remove those who have nothing to say except repetitive negativity and discrimination? Is there anyone out there who can speak out to big companies and the government to place stricter policies on social media platforms? This, I cannot say, but it is something for you to think about.

Are you at all interested in fashion? We all want to look good to feel good, but have you ever thought about the issues that fashionistas are struggling with? Well, deciding what to wear on an occasion is one thing, but have you ever thought about the issues with fast fashion? When it comes to viral outfits, everybody wants to wear it at a cheap, thin price. A price just like the material bought on a cheap website. How can we prevent this in the future? Will these websites get shut down? When can we wear whatever we want without being put down? When will we realise fashion trends are wasteful to the economy and our town? This, I cannot say, but it is something for you to think about.

Look down at your town once more. What do you see? Are there better facilities to suit everyone's needs? Is there more than a world where robots rule supreme?

I shall not be here next time you come. The future is up to you, not I.

You might see things differently here, but never be afraid to give things a try.

For the future is for sightseeing risk-takers, resilient and free.

The future is however you want to make it, not me.

The power is in your hands and yours only, my friend,
So make the most of your surroundings and belongings until the end.
The choice is entirely yours, my friend.

———————————

Hello, my name is LILY HARRISON and I am a student from Newfriars College in Stoke-on-Trent. Our specialist college is THE place for students aged 16-25, as they are supported by our phenomenal team of colleagues and staff who help them to gain independent living skills in preparation for adulthood.

I am in my third year of college and I am currently studying Photography and AS Level English. I would like to think that my friends and family view me as a bright and creative young lady. In my spare time, I enjoy reading, writing, baking and, most importantly, self-care.

NEWFRIARS COLLEGE is an Independent Specialist Day College in Stoke-On-Trent dedicated to supporting young people with Special Educational Needs and Disabilities aged between 16–25. Our aim is to transform the lives of young people through partnership, collaboration, enterprise and innovation. Our vision is to maximise opportunities within the community and provide a breadth and richness of experience that enables all our learners to reach their full potential and be part of an inclusive society.

SIDRA HUSEJNOVIC

Nottingham Academy

The Town of the Future will be enhanced, the children will have a never-ending thought of entranced, while our town romanced human validation and the glory of finance, why can't our town take a chance?

The youth of this generation know no better, and our propriety is based on what area we are from; the society we have created is like an insulated balloon that is indicated to blow up soon, while the adults in the room watch the party knowing they must stop us but they're waiting for the results to come up soon.

Let me not forget the silent screams that our town is dealing with, by all means the NHS losing their jobs. We are also facing a high rate of homelessness and the MP is doing all she can, but we know they are hopeless and soon going to be roadless if we carry on letting them sleep on the streets.

But The Town of the Future will soon develop, we won't see post code wars or outdoor four on four fights over who owns who's sights. The new generation will open their eyes and see the grand prize that the town holds. The town isn't prominent yet, but it will be dominant.

Although it's not normal for another town to drown like ours do, we won the crown for the most crimes around and no one can't seem to find a way to stop them. We have youngsters stab Olders over exposures and disclosures. Do you not see the problem?

Lets not fail to recall the passion our town gives, the fashion we wear and we swear there's love behind the hatred, we defiantly care. Our community helps each other out at every opportunity we can, and the town is small but the walls are tall and that's all we need for now.

———————————

My name is **SIDRA HUSEJNOVIC** and I'm 16 years old. I have a passion for business and finance but the main career goal I would like to achieve is being a commercial pilot. My hobbies out of school are spoken word, reading and planning how to succeed in my goals.

NOTTINGHAM
ACADEMY

NOTTINGHAM ACADEMY is a non-selective school for students in Nottingham. Through an inspirational curriculum we facilitate great learning, exceptional progress and the development of character. We ensure all pupils achieve their potential and are ready for the next stage in their learning, training, or employment.

DANIEL JONES

The Skinners' School

The Town of the Future will be one built and centred around a smart town hub; incorporated into the landscape, taking advantage of renewable energy sources and ensuring an abundance of green space. This will be done whilst focused on sustaining maximum social and economic welfare; being instigated through a social cohesive framework intertwined with technological systems.

A town being regenerative is fundamental to its sustainable existence, it is not enough to be net zero. The future will require towns to be fuelled purely by renewables through the implementation of solar, wind, geothermal and biomass sources that are all non-geographically specific. The means of storage (of energy) will be requisite through the use of batteries and fuel cells to maximise efficiency and flexibility of distribution. In addition, with the use of renewable sources and effective storage, it would mean all towns would be able to operate as an isolated unit from the national grid, producing all energy on site if needed. A resultant surplus of energy could be established, which would mitigate impacts of a crisis. A surplus would also allow for future carrying capacity to be increased whilst remaining in the walls of regenerative design. This is because the flexible energy system would allow for easy distribution for growth and town enhancement, with low opportunity costs. As well as the attainment of energy, the built environment will also maximise natural light and minimise the requirement for artificial light. Moreover, the built environment, using materials which significantly reduce heat loss as well as utilizing natural light, results in reduced requirement for input energy.

Water in the future will be scarce and therefore its allocation, utilization and management are essential for staying in the bounds of the regenerative framework. Multiple steps must be added to the water's consumption cycle; greywater needing to be managed and recycled effectively, being implemented everywhere potable water isn't necessary (decreasing wastewater or excessive treatment). The conditions under which water management will be executed is based in blue-green infrastructure (BGI), incorporating the town into the natural water cycle. Green sustainable drainage solutions can reduce flood risk. BGI also increases the amount of green space which is fundamental for carbon sequestration, improved air quality and biodiversity benefits.

Improved water management, as well as mitigating against water related hazards will also reduce the exigency for grey infrastructure. Another element of the town's water management will be the rationing controls combining with a streamlined distribution system, ensuring the supply of water is allocatively efficient. In terms of sewage, future towns will have implemented schemes in order to minimise wastewater run-off, to treat and eradicate the negative externalities of sewage dumps and particularly the effect sewage has on the biodiversity of surrounding areas. Finally, potable water will be sourced through a system of rainwater channels and maximising the naturally available potable water, resulting in less demand for external sources.

The means by which self-sufficiency is achieved is through community co-operation and smart city technology. Therefore, the towns of the future will utilize the 'Internet of Things' where objects and town locations are all interconnected through software and adapt their operating function to suit the town's needs. The presence of a central community hub for local government, as well as the centre of the interconnected web of technology, will enhance the strive to create a healthy living environment that can easily be sustained for future generations. This expedites the sharing of information allowing for co-operation to be accomplished through knowledge commons. This sharing of knowledge benefits consumers, as it erodes the information gap between economic agents allowing for optimal economic utility; this eradicates market force inefficiencies meaning consumers can still maximise economic welfare. As well as knowledge, smart mobility promotes efficient transport to eradicate congestion and increases individuals' ease of movement. The town will become a mass negative feedback system in which social, economic and environmental inefficiencies and inequalities will be corrected. This will equip a community with the ability to narrow focus onto the main goal of encouraging the trinity of mental, physical and social health, through emphasising access to sport and green infrastructure. It is all being part of the composition for socialisation, to encourage the integration of all peoples, creating greater town unity and welfare.

Overall, The Town of the Future will take advantage of not just the natural but also human capital, optimising available resources, whilst remaining embedded in the regenerative and smart framework. "It is a way of being in the world that embraces biosphere stewardship and recognises that we have a responsibility to leave the living world in a better state than we found it" (Kate Raworth).

DANIEL JONES: I study Economics, Geography, Maths and Further Maths at A Level. I enjoy reading about economics, particularly behavioural economics, the implications of economic actions on communities and individuals, as well as international development. I follow current affairs and geopolitical issues. I am also a keen sportsman playing football and tennis.

THE SKINNERS' SCHOOL is a selective Grammar School in Tunbridge Wells. It was first opened in 1887. The current roll is 1,119, with 325 in the Sixth Form. Skinners' aims to achieve academic excellence for all its pupils, whilst at the same time developing their independence as learners. There is a strong focus on learning outside the classroom, through co-curricular and extra-curricular activity, in particular preparing pupils for life beyond school including the expectation they will play a significant role in their communities and in society as a whole.

SHANIA KEMBLE

New College Swindon

T he Town of the Future will have made major advances in saving our planet. Electric monorails will be set up to run to all major areas, making the streets safe for pedestrians and commuters alike because there will be fewer vehicles on the road. This will be a large part of cutting down our carbon emissions and halting climate change, as these do not emit carbon. All houses will be built, as standard, with air conditioning to combat the rising temperatures in the UK summers. Solar panels are fitted to save money on electric bills and lower our carbon emissions even further. With electric car chargers fitted in all homes and in public places, petrol will have become obsolete. Most cars drive themselves, so the passengers will have more free time to complete work or sit back and relax.

The town centre will no longer be a place of shopping for clothes or gifts. This has already started moving online and will continue doing so. Instead, it will be a place for experiences and socialisation. The centre will be filled with entertainment venues and activities. Restaurants that take you on a virtual journey to new lands. Imagine walking into a Thai restaurant and feeling like you have been transported to Thailand itself. The walls have become screens and take you on a tour of the beautiful country of Thailand, where you not only see the place, but you also smell the flowers and spices around you. People can already order food from any takeaway easily and have any food they want. People need a reason to go out and this would give them a sense of adventure and excitement. These restaurants, as well as every other establishment, will have menus in braille and be fully accessible to wheelchairs and mobility scooters. Our society will be inclusive, and equality will be paramount.

Many of the materials that we use for building will work towards reducing our carbon footprint and becoming waste-free. Insulation for houses will be made from mycelium, the vegetative part of mushrooms. This is completely natural, biodegradable and considerably reduces the carbon footprint of the average house. Chipboard for use in making furniture and buildings will be created from discarded potato scraps that previously would have been wasted. Cement currently accounts for 5% of global carbon emissions so, to reduce this, zero-cement concrete will instead be used, all without compromising the strength of the buildings. It can be laid up to ten times faster than conventional concrete which will help speed up the time it takes to create new buildings too.

Virtual reality will be a major part of our entertainment. The technology will only continue advancing and those who once would not have been able to afford to travel and try new sports or activities will find themselves with access to everything they have ever dreamed of. There will be countless new venues dedicated to bringing these dreams to life. By placing on a headset and standing on a treadmill that moves in whatever direction you do, people will find themselves thrown into the middle of an African safari, or scuba-diving in the Great Barrier Reef. It will feel as real as if you were there yourself. Virtual reality will also be revolutionary for schooling. Poorer countries will be able to access top-quality education from abroad and students can see 3D models to aid learning. They will also be able to experience destinations without leaving the classroom.

Major medical advancements will be made, and these will be widely available to everyone. Senses that have been impaired will be able to be restored to perfect function by chips implanted. Imagine a cochlear implant to give you perfect hearing or a retinal implant to give you perfect eyesight. Damaged tissue and organs will be able to be repaired, with life-saving new treatments. Food shortages will be fixed by artificially growing all types of foods, from lab-grown meat to artificially created milk. Extra nutrients and vitamins can be added to combat deficiencies.

More wind turbines will be placed at sea to harness the power of the wind and to create another renewable source of energy that will have a substantially lower impact on the environment than burning fossil fuels. Hydropower will be used alongside these other methods to cover any vulnerabilities that solar and wind power has. Hydropower will make it possible to react quickly to any increases in demand of power, as the intake of water can be increased, or extra generators brought online.

I envision a town that is a place of innovation and diversity. A place for everyone to thrive and enjoy being a part of. The Town of the Future will be one I want to live in.

SHANIA KEMBLE: I am studying English Language and Literature at A Level and I love writing whenever I get the chance to! I am passionate about reading fiction, especially science fiction and fantasy books. I enjoy listening to and playing all genres of music.

NEW COLLEGE SWINDON: Whatever the need, we are here to help our students achieve their goals and guide them on their paths. Really, they are ones that inspire us and give us the motivation to try our hardest. Thank you for aiding us in this endeavour.

LUCY MANN

Chestnut Grove Academy

The Town of the Future will be…

Loved like a new born child.
Overgrown with stems of buildings.
Switched on with the sun's glare.
Tired of promises. And regrets.

Hidden with history.
Electrified by oceans.
Limited to two more weeks.
Put on display for Pluto.
Left to support all creatures.
Eaten by concrete.
Scared to burst into polluted air.
Saved by drops of ice sweat.

The Town of the Future will be...

Washed away with dust.
Artificial forests on a screen, pixilated green.
Slaughtered by drills and saws.
Thought of as a 'victory'.
Explored by potential buyers.
Drenched in Diesel.

Manipulated to admire its creation.
Addicted to carbon dioxide.
New to our parenting method.
Motivated to shoot... not protect.
Avoidant of physical touch. Love. And trust.
Deprived from sleep.
Expected to survive Storm Social Media.

The Town of the Future will be gone before we have it.

———————————

My name is LUCY MANN, and I'm 16 years old. At the Chestnut Grove Sixth-Form, I study English Literature, Media and Performing Arts, which I am interested in pursuing in the future. Studying English has enabled me to analyse many poems and become influenced by critiquing society through hidden meanings.

CHESTNUT GROVE ACADEMY prides itself on providing a creative learning community by ensuring that students have a rigorous, knowledge rich, transformational education encapsulated through our PROUD values, which prepares our students to succeed at university, thrive in employment and lead fulfilling lives. Our values are also underpinned by the UN Convention of the rights of the child. For this reason, Chestnut Grove is a rights-respecting school in which staff and students actively advocate for the rights of others.

SOPHIE MCGILLICUDDY

Brentside High School

The Town of the Future will be different than now
The winds will change and the grass somehow,
Will consistently grow and consistently be cut
And unfortunately our current community will someday be shut.

But,
There's a hope that still resides
That maybe one day civilisation will stand side by side
That matters will be fought and inequality will be rare
Mistreating one another will float away like air.

My friends will be able to love whoever they prefer,
Without getting stares, or threats, or slurs.
I hope these will be no more than a distant memory
And everyone, and I mean everyone, will be welcoming of their ceremony.

My nephew will hopefully grow up in a world better than my own,

One more mature and intellectually grown.
I pray he isn't discriminated against because of his race,
And people will see him as no more than a smiling face.

I know deep down there's an immense chance this won't be the case,
As I already know how difficult that is the human race,
How small minded a person can really be
And how unpleasant the world can really seem.

But,
There is still a chance that change could happen
There is just a lot to improve before it's begun.
I know this sounds like a cliche poem,
However at least I'm trying to do something as well as at least show them.

Please though, for our sake don't wait,
This is our chance to change our world's state.
To change our climate crisis as well as change the worlds views,
And change corruption that the world continues to pursue.

———————

SOPHIE MCGILLICUDDY: I have always been interested in writing and being creative and love to share my work with my friends and family. I want to continue to hone my creativity in the future and challenge myself even further to see what other types of art I can possibly produce.

BRENTSIDE HIGH SCHOOL is an inner-city London comprehensive with a very high pupil premium intake and most children speaking English as their second language.

IQRA MOHAMMED

Trafford College

The Town of the Future will forever be ours till the end of time, as we all grow to be victorious. Moreover we will grow to be successful, even powerful to those who tried to stand before us, take down our home and ruin us by risking everyone's lives in danger for all ages. As we all unite together yelping out their options as well as opinions on how we would love to live our life with no problems whatsoever.

One elderly citizen shouted from the crowd one interesting point: "No violence like gun fights physical abuse or domestic violence should be present; if it happens punishment must be in place for those individuals!" No one should be tortured for a problem they weren't involved or took action alongside as it was never their fault to start with.

Second public citizen screeching out: "Young children and teenagers should be free to do whatever they want!" But with limits. Furthermore, to achieve all of this, the teenagers should be taught by their responsible parents as it is compulsory that they should have the mindset of an adult to visit overcrowded public places to be aware of what is being preceded or what would take place in their surroundings.

Third, public citizens have been heard: "We all deserve free WiFi and no taxes need to be paid except for the forces in charge (Governments/Politicians). They would handle all the payments but will share it when it's needed to whoever is in need of money for necessary resources along with services. Money will need to be given back if it has been misused incorrectly as that payment could be used for other resources like shelter, food, cars, medicines, etc.

Fourth, public citizens spoke out explaining: "Hate crime should be ended as well as treating everyone the same equally with no disrespect given back to them". This could end if everyone paused against their grudges by letting it all out peacefully with no physical actions needed to be used but just talk it out like exactly how pride people who would respect each other dignity with truce and no false answers.

The Town of the Future finally ready to be our will forever as sun will keep shining its way down to Earth, showering its warmness expressing positive energy for all humans. Until rain will shatters down causing the ground to turn into smoke as gas makes it through the ground melting as they're slipping away destroying all moods and emotions of a human being making them lose control of their beloved towns as it drains away into hole nowhere to be seen and found again.

My name is **IQRA MOHAMMED** and I'm 17 years old. In my free time I would love to talk to people worldwide as it's very fascinating to know what their countries are like compared to our country but through their perspective. I sometimes would research random topics which I don't really need to know but find interesting to know them in future references. I love to make random stories or short raps in my head when everything is silent as it sounds completely more funny than when it's written on paper. I would never need inspiration from anything I see as I just write whatever is in my head on to a piece of paper and let everything flow into a piece becoming a story or an essay. Inspiration is all around you, we just need to find it through our own eyes and make it into our own words but never feel afraid or shy of what others will think when they read it.

TRAFFORD COLLEGE is a further education college with 5 different campuses. We thrive to provide an inclusive educational offer that serves the needs of our local community for young people and adult learners; and to provide a careers focused curriculum that meets the needs of local businesses, and enables our students to further their employment prospects. In short, we are here to ensure our students develop the skills, attitudes and behaviours required for success in life and work.

PHILIP NORUWA

Lambeth Academy

RUINATION

The Town of the Future will not have to endure the pain we experience now. I remember moments before the disaster when hundreds of twisted wooden limbs reached towards the skies like a child beseeching for help. I remember the shucking of sequoias; their precious bark about to be incinerated into worthless pieces of dust. I remember the lolling leaves bowing their heads in hopelessness as they realised, they were going to be partakers in the tragic fate of the upcoming hazard. Every tree is different from the brown mahoganies to the coast redwoods but one thing they all had in common was that they couldn't escape the chaos that was about to take place. Beneath, thousands of strands of grass swayed back and forth, back and forth trembling at the mere thought of being uprooted. The cold wind taunted the vulnerable greenery by serving as a never ending reminder that they are approaching the end of their short lives.

As evening approached and heavens faded into a vantablack hue, the sun quivered beneath the horizon, as if it were grateful for the opportune moment it had to elude the upcoming tragedy. The stoic grace of the moon was nowhere to be found along with the usual stars of light. In the centre of the redwood biome, lounged an insatiable viscous creature, whose magma floundered their way about this beast. Its fissures were its veins. Its body was enveloped in layers of cragged grey strata. It had no compassionate soul, lacked consideration and served no utilitarian purpose other than to cause setback and destruction to mankind. Eternally open, its circular mouth laid dormant, impatient for its soon eructation of lava and to become the provocation of chaos. In time, the magma arose. We were unprepared. The magma brimmed. We were fearful. The magma erupted. We were ruined.

Those were many months ago.

Even now, it has become natural for tears to meander their way about the cheeks of our people – a relief from all the suffering. It is said that a picture paints a thousand words, and this was no different. Eroded by grief, our sepia eyes were cast to the ground as we currently lacked the motivation to thrive and rebuild. A frown had chosen to temporarily reside on our faces and thirstful, sore throats were now commonplace, likewise the solace of food and water quickly became a longing luxury. Our way of life and our culture had been disfigured, the intricate buildings of my home Pheouric were unrecognisable, transforming its beauty into fragmented, rubble of no value. Despite all of this, I will remain still hopeful that:

The Town of the Future will be better.

————————————

PHILIP NORUWA: At university I would like to study Physics because I am passionate about mechanics such as kinematics and waves and how this could be used in real life situations. I like non-fiction because I am able to learn more about abstract concepts such as the theory of Time Dilation.

LAMBETH ACADEMY is a thriving school in the heart of London. We are proud of our rigorous curriculum and high-quality teaching. We focus on 'education with character', one that challenges, inspires and excites students and provides a rich variety of opportunities both inside and outside of the classroom. We are confident that when you visit us you will see students and staff exhibiting our three core values of Commitment to Progress, Excellence in Thinking and Honourable Leadership.

AYOMIDE OLU-DAVIES

St Ambrose Barlow RC High School

The Town of the Future is what we make it,
It depends on what we do.
We could change our ways and make things better,
So our grandkids won't have to.

We can tackle industrialisation and waste
To rid us of pollution
We can optimise our energy
And develop a solution.

With public transport and solar panels
We can make our cities greener.
We will recycle our water and reduce our waste
To make our cities cleaner.

The Town of the Future may bring despair
If we don't take a stand,
If net carbon doesn't drop to zero,
Our issues will expand.

The skies will get dirtier and the air will get thicker.
The ozone layer will deteriorate quicker.

The natural world will suffer, the animals and ice caps,
While our actions cause civilisations to collapse.
Where there was greenery, waste will be,
Sealife will suffer as plastic fills the sea.

We could make things better with the things we invent
We could tackle homelessness and unemployment.
We could live in a world filled with nature and trees
Or exist in a hell where we live with unease.
The Town of the Future could go either way,
We could do nothing as our towns decay
Or we act now and pave the way
We can make our towns sustainable
Or the effects will be irreversible.

———————————

My name is **AYOMIDE OLU-DAVIES**. I'm 16 years old and I hope to have a career in the real estate sector. My friends would say I am ambitious, driven and always eager and excited to learn. I try to put 100% effort into everything I do.

ST AMBROSE BARLOW RC HIGH SCHOOL: We are an 11-16 Catholic community school of faith where it is a privilege to see our young people flourishing, to speak with them, to learn their ways and watch them grow in confidence. There is great spirit and energy in this school. You can see it in the range of extra-curricular activities, in the array of research projects undertaken by staff and in the creativity that flows through our learning. We thrive on connections: with parents and carers, with parishes, with businesses. We love to look out and give our pupils a global perspective on learning. By doing this our students can see a higher purpose in their learning.

ANIYA PRAMANIK

London Academy of Excellence

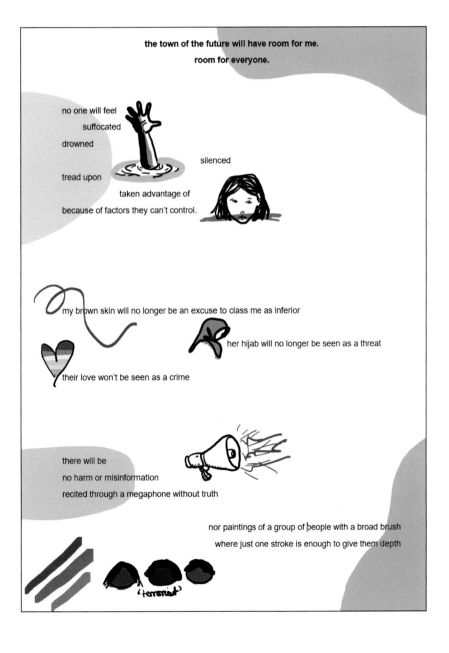

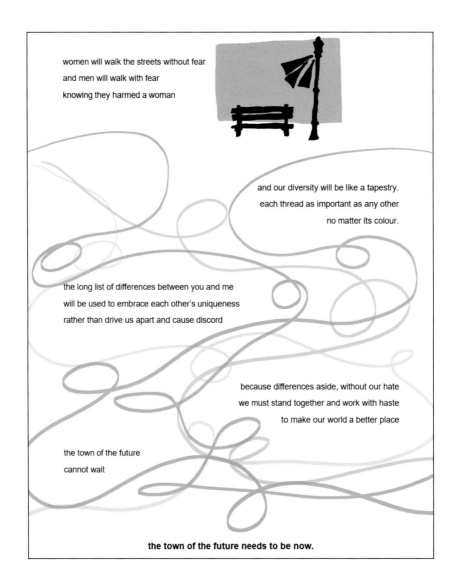

women will walk the streets without fear
and men will walk with fear
knowing they harmed a woman

and our diversity will be like a tapestry.
each thread as important as any other
no matter its colour.

the long list of differences between you and me
will be used to embrace each other's uniqueness
rather than drive us apart and cause discord

because differences aside, without our hate
we must stand together and work with haste
to make our world a better place

the town of the future
cannot wait

the town of the future needs to be now.

ANIYA PRAMANIK is a Year 12 student from East London, who is passionate about a wide range of interests from learning languages to writing songs and playing gigs under the stage name Hazy Sofia. She also enjoys knitting, crocheting, and doodling in her spare time. This piece was written about a theme that is deeply important to Aniya: identity and belonging.

The **LONDON ACADEMY OF EXCELLENCE** is one of the highest-performing sixth form colleges in the United Kingdom and an engine of social mobility. LAE consistently delivers outstanding A level results for all students but has achieved particular success helping students from less advantaged backgrounds gain places at the finest universities in the UK and around the world.

UMAYYA RAHMAN

London Academy of Excellence

TOWN

The Town of the Future will move on
advance as we must
but,
could i have the same fate
may i have the same fate?

it's wild right
because

i still love you.

i want to be your source of comfort,
your stress relief, your little bubble.
your sun and moon and stars all in one
i want to be the town of your future,
i want to be your everything.

when i meant something to you,
i meant something for me too.
i wouldn't be able to find that feeling with anyone else i don't
want to find that feeling with anyone else.

perhaps you are like my town

the town of my past;
a cinema where i can escape to another reality
a playground where i can let loose the child in me
a shop where i have everything i need

a pharmacy where everything is available to fix me
a counselling centre where i wont be judged
a mental asylum where i can get the help i may need

and
a home.
simply where i can feel at home.

could that be my future too?

wipe the tears away and suddenly see

a future where it never suns,
birds no longer chirping
silence.
flowers refuse to blossom as though
it does not belong to them.

bad weather is a norm
hurricanes, tsunamis, thunder, lightning, pollution, dependency, infatuation,
obsession.

crime unleashes one day and
the police are our heroes

but at the end of the day it is still
a never-ending cycle

though
like town fog,
you are blurry in my mind now.
and now i have never feared
such a sight,
of when the skies turn grey.
breaking
into small pieces
but i still choose to believe
i can be mended in our towns repair shop

so is this really the future I want

its ok,
i sleep now knowing i'll be able to see you. even if i see you with someone else
at least i can still see you.

weird how I have that same exact dream every single day.

UMAYYA RAHMAN: I am an ambitious individual who aspires to help as many as I can in the future. I enjoy exploring my creative side by writing poetry where I can express my feelings on certain viewpoints and topics, which is aided by my love for reading fictional literature.

The **LONDON ACADEMY OF EXCELLENCE** is one of the highest-performing sixth form colleges in the United Kingdom and an engine of social mobility. LAE consistently delivers outstanding A level results for all students but has achieved particular success helping students from less advantaged backgrounds gain places at the finest universities in the UK and around the world.

OLSHA
RODRIGUES

St Mark's Catholic School

As our loving God of Peace blessed the birthing aura of sanctity drifting upon a cleansing land, a clear cascade of liquefied purity washes away the iniquities that lay upon a sin-stained shore as the earth is purged of its suffering.

The Town of the Future will be set free once again – free from the vociferating roars of the wind. The screeching chuckles of taunting trees. The choking grasp of quicksand. The crimson red ruins that society once trudged through consisted of a morbid easel of pitch black emptiness – a dark page in the history of humanity's collective story.

The history books will look back to the age of sadness and despondency, a time when life was caged and bedarkened in blindness.

Bedarkened with the cataclysm of a sorrowful palette, the primordial monstrosity of entwining muddy veins, once a beautiful tree, drowned in the deluge of nature's overthrow. The labyrinth of malady-brown and diseased threaded roots of grime twisted incomprehensibly into a wiry malformation as it wrenched a wooden body – in a predatory manner – tight in its grasp, ensnaring it with the inducement of liquid necessities. Violently, scars on the victimised body of the sepia-brown tree ripped open with age, whilst its damp and decaying corpse bred a malodorous, acrid miasma. Death loomed. It struggled to breathe as merciless mud and water seeped into every crook and carving that grew on its surface as it lay vulnerable on the saturated ground and diminished. The roots had choked. The tree was gone.

Bobbing streams that bore the portals to the heart of the earth once gently coursed through a solitary yet calm and composed existence but the defiance and neglect of supposed 'stewards' of the world, slowly caused the gentility of the streams and lakes to topple into a liquid rage.

Bottomless cauldrons of burning fluid fuelled by an ancient wrath, bubbling and boiling, encroached every last inch of life that was left unadulterated. A stinging smell of pungent petrichor cascaded through the callously devouring indigo rivulet – a liquid anaconda. The hideous reflection of the cosmic battle in the sky preceded a thunderous yell from the clouds as yet again, the foreboding procession of falling leaves fractured the river; the liquid snake shivered in apprehension – a chaotic calamity. Beneath the tearful sky, the storm whipped the river as it flooded with uncontrollable sorrow.

The flooding of the river mirrored the overflow of metanoia in the hearts of society and as the earth trampled towards the mirage of hope, a drop of sunshine healed the despair as a blessing beckoned from beyond the sombre wintry hues of barrenness – the answer to a reverent prayer had arrived as unswerving tears of mercy dropped from the Heavenly Abode of God and a flicker of light, blossomed.

Metamorphosis.

Serenity. Soul soothing peace stroked the lingering aura of Eden-like beauty with a soft nudge of familial love. Faint traces of the bruised remnants of the tree revitalised as they caught the glory of the rising sun, congealing into the glistening aqua blue beauty as a splendorous foretaste of Heaven. Watchful guardians of the forest nodded and swayed in the motion of the wind and beckoned towards a casket of olive green luxury. Lulled by the frigid, tickling wind, lilac butterflies journeyed along the rejuvenating liquid carpet to a caramel discovery beyond the trove of cobalt treasuries where there stood the wise, hazel body of a new tree that outreached branches of viridescent leaves. The nostalgic traces of legacy and charm adorned the mysteriously entwined being, as it stroked the skies and stood proud in its roots encasing the poetry of the scenes in an everlasting emerald green embrace. The tree was revived.

A musical breeze caressed a dribble of synchronised ripples that vivaciously bobbed in the serene azure river that was replenished from its former misery. The honey crest of a sun congealed into the liquid blanket – a truthful reflection of the Amazing Grace above, whilst beholding the mirror image of porcelain-white tipped mountains, stirring gently in the river's motion. Sprouts of aquatic green mossy marshes dribbled in the realms of an aquamarine mirage as an orchestra of birdsong beamed at the ultramarine river's serenity.

Beauty was restored and The Town of the Future was healed through Love.

My name is **OLSHA RODRIGUES**, I am 17 years old and I am a student of St Mark's Catholic School. I wrote this short story as an illustration of the world today and I believe that through love, we can eradicate the negativity that plagues our common home.

ST MARK'S CATHOLIC SCHOOL is an 11-18 co-educational Catholic school in Hounslow, West London with over 1,200 students. The school is founded on the Christian values, expressed in the gospels: peace, truth, justice and love. St. Mark's is a truly inclusive community and we celebrate our pupils' achievements, together with providing outstanding pastoral support. St. Mark's enjoys an outstanding reputation for academic achievement based on a consistent record of excellent examination results.

FATIMA SHARIF

Lambeth Academy

ERODING TIME

T he Town of the Future will be built with their wreckful, twisting words which are concealed as lies after they have proven themselves with their display of the past. They remain shattered as glass pieces – which carefully placed together reveal the horror of the war they started. Time was not a friend either as each second spent in that barren, bleak place surged his nostrils with a deep pungent smell of the rotten corpses. He trod carefully, trying to not further disfigure and break them however this proved to be a challenge as the dark underworld beneath the sticky ground surfaces constantly attempted to grip his shoes beneath to where everyone else is.

The wind danced in spirals as the sky was swollen with tears. This sucked the life out of the once vibrant painted sky which used to make the people of Keem hopeful of tomorrow's forthcomings. Dark coloured grey clouds mingled in groups and hung like a blanket around the city turned battlefield and suffocated the air and trapped heat. Sweat dribbled down his stern face which are creased of hardly earned wrinkles, so he gulps down nearly half of his water he carries in his neatly organised travel bag. Afterall, while travelling he was warned about the eye-wrenching scenes of Keem as he needs to pass it to reach Delim, where he would be able to sell the jewellery he made from the stones and jewels he collected from the town before.

Silence echoed into the vast wasteland which rang in Delan's ears. Suddenly, Delan's horse neighed loudly which shattered the stiffening silence. He was confused as he was told nobody from Keem survived the attack. Delan looked around and carefully walked over to where his horse was which was next to an abandoned home. Curious, he walked into the stripped home to find a seemingly young boy which was as small as a post stamp.

FATIMA SHARIF: My favourite author is Franz Kafka as his writing helped me to evaluate life situations and deal with reality's glass ceilings. The recurring resilience of his main characters, which strive to defeat the situation they're in, and are constantly drowned in hope is an attitude, I think we need in life to achieve our best. Currently, I am reading 'Klara and the Sun' by Kazou Ishiguro. My favourite book of all time is 'Mornings in Jenin' by Susan Abulhaw.

LAMBETH ACADEMY is a thriving school in the heart of London. We are proud of our rigorous curriculum and high-quality teaching. We focus on 'education with character', one that challenges, inspires and excites students and provides a rich variety of opportunities both inside and outside of the classroom. We are confident that when you visit us you will see students and staff exhibiting our three core values of Commitment to Progress, Excellence in Thinking and Honourable Leadership.

ANGELINA SHIJU

St Mark's Catholic School

THE TOWN OF THE FUTURE WILL BE RAMSHACKLE

They say a future so bright and blissful
But if only we saw it to be true,
For the days are discontent as if holding a pistol
Ruthless use of power, no happiness left to pursue

We told them the domain be kept verdant green
We told them to reprocess and not waste,
For now the globe is achromic, with inferno at the very scene
Masses of H_2O but no marine life to be showcased

I thought it would be better, with mindsets eager to assist
200 storey buildings along with pretty flying spaceships -
But to think technology was there once; now there's no mammals to exist
A home to once 8 billion, now a polluted party house with no relationships.

But it could have been different with less consumption, enjoying bright blue skies. If you'd stop before you throw your can in the river, making sure another fish won't die!

––––––––––––––––––––

ANGELINA SHIJU: I am an A Level student who is fascinated by the future since it is unavoidable, and the best way to foresee it is to repair what we have wrecked and create what is good. We are accountable not just for giving ourselves the life we want, but also for leaving a legacy for others.

ST MARK'S CATHOLIC SCHOOL is an 11-18 co-educational Catholic school in Hounslow, West London with over 1,200 students. The school is founded on the Christian values, expressed in the gospels: peace, truth, justice and love. St. Mark's is a truly inclusive community and we celebrate our pupils' achievements, together with providing outstanding pastoral support. St. Mark's enjoys an outstanding reputation for academic achievement based on a consistent record of excellent examination results.

SANTOSH SOLOMON

Futures Institute Banbury

The Town of the Future will fall into despair because of him.

Once, there was a small town called Trixtent. The town was filled with the best of the best from all over the world. It was the most modern, independent and civilised town at that time. Only the top 1% was able to apply for residency and only 20 people get accepted every year. Once your application gets declined you can't apply again for another decade. If you're one of the lucky ones and get accepted you are greeted to luxury. Luxury which you cannot buy. People can get whatever they want whenever they want it.

On one faithful Saturday evening when the moon was brighter than usual, a baby was born who was named Bazua Dos Santos. He was born in the most ordinary way, which was in a test tube. He was the only child family. His father was a doctor and his mother was also a doctor. He was an abnormal child since he was young, he was unable to grasp every concept he was taught. He learnt to write his name at the age 10. He then learnt basic maths at the age of 15. By the age of 20 he learnt to have a basic conversation. Although it took him decades to learn the basics, he had mastered every concept he came across by the age of 21. Many people had said he had mastered life at 25 years old. He had earnt a total of 5 Nobel prizes over the course of 5 years. In those 5 years, He would come up with new theory equation every month and new theory every other week.

On his 26th birthday, Bazua had become the youngest quadrillionare, this meant he was eligible to apply for residency in Trixtent. Although his success was acknowledged by normal civilians, it wasn't acknowledged by the trixtent citizens. They thought that he was a fluke and that he got lucky and some believed that all he said were lies, some even didn't know who he was. A week later he sent his application; he got his results. He was not accepted. The trixtent citizens vote for who they want in their country. He had only applied because his parents told him to. Bazua didn't actually want to live in Trixtent; this was because of how they treated their workers. Although to get to live there you need to be part of the 1%, to work there you don't need to. The workers weren't considered as people in Trixtent because they didn't earn it. The workers might not have been part of the 1% but they were the best of the best.

To punish the people of Trixtent Bazua had thought of a prank for the residents. He would build a nuclear bomb and fake a nuclear attack for rejecting his offer. He started to build it and he told his friends to spread the news so people could hear it. After a week everyone in every part of the world heard about this and started panicking that they might be caught in the cross fire. He also built a plane to fly over Trixtent. He was planning on pranking them in a month's time.

His game plan was to fly over Trixtent and fake it. He thought nothing could go wrong and that was his biggest mistake. He started his plane and went over Trixtent, just before he got there, he thought he heard sharp windy noise, but he just forgot about it and carried on. When he was over Trixtent he was sniped in the head. He collapsed and dropped the bomb...

SANTOSH SOLOMON: I was brought up in India and came to the UK when I was 8. I chose to come to Futures Institute as I wanted to study Computer Science and Engineering. I'm not sure what I want to do for my future career yet, it may even be in finance.

FUTURES INSTITUTE BANBURY is a specialist STEM school and part of the Aspirations Academies Trust. Students often come to our school because of their interest in technology and our unique curriculum which has a focus on transdisciplinary learning. In years 9 & 10 we run specific employability projects in different areas including health; environment; design and engineering. These projects aim to develop 21st century skills that will be vital to our students in the workplace such as teamwork and creativity – all the projects also aim to link to employers.

MARIAM VAZIRY

Lambeth Academy

CANVAS LASSIES, CHEF-D'OEUVRE

The Town of the Future, will they look the other way?
When a lassie pulls at her skirt, plain and grey
'No menacing grins,' she asks softly
Though they stare relentlessly, occasionally whistling
Let the lassie's hair flow on her bare shoulders, I ask
Do not smoulder her with unwanted looks or touch, I warn
'Replace my trembling hands at dark with yours, ones that can protect me,' she pleads
For all that, they do not listen. Feet away from her, leering.

Her body, an untouched vessel blooms, like bulbs at week three
Be that as it may, its growth wore out, on March 2nd
What was, was no more.
They hear but do not listen;
Eyes but no ears?
With gentle fingers, she unveils her frail canvas
Her arms and hips and waist and breasts and stomach and thighs and neck. Softly,
she asks, 'do you remember?'
They hear but do not listen
'Is my canvas pretty?' she asks, cold colours purple and blue, 'Look,'
She points
'What beautiful art you've made, you must be so talented for it only took an hour or
two.' She turns her head, 'Oh, The Town of the Future,' she groans
'Hang me up in museums, let the world know of my artist's masterpiece. All these
colours!' 'Place me among the rest of his works, allow the town to see me, like all the
ones before.' And so, she was.

The townspeople glorified his work, honouring each one with photographs and
compliments Canvas lassies was what they called them

Each art piece hung by a by a rusted nail; their message heavier though disdained
With droopy eyes I turned look, her golden hair still untouched

I tried to help the poor lassie, but nobody would hear, nobody would listen. There've been many canvas lassies before her

For I was and am one too
Perhaps there will be more to come
Or will The Town of the Future decide to listen?
Will they look away instead?

———————

MARIAM VAZIRY: I live in London where I study English Literature as part of my three a-levels at my sixth form. I enjoy American novels such as 'The Great Gatsby', plays like 'A Doll's House' and poetry written by Christina Rossetti. I am currently completing an extra-curricular project activity on 'Shakespeare's Restless World' written by Neil MacGregor.

LAMBETH ACADEMY is a thriving school in the heart of London. We are proud of our rigorous curriculum and high-quality teaching. We focus on 'education with character', one that challenges, inspires and excites students and provides a rich variety of opportunities both inside and outside of the classroom. We are confident that when you visit us you will see students and staff exhibiting our three core values of Commitment to Progress, Excellence in Thinking and Honourable Leadership.

SHORT
ESSAYS

BY

 # INDUSTRY
LEADERS

SIMON ALLFORD

Allford Hall Monaghan Morris

The Town of the Future will be both very different and very familiar. History tells us that. For images of the future are always trapped in the present. That also explains why any alien in the history of storytelling is instantly recognisable as either human, animal, invertebrate or a combination thereof. My view is informed by a study of the past and a talk I enjoy giving titled 'A brief history of the future': the predictions of the future always overplay change - buildings will walk, or fly, or we will be flown to them, or even teleported.

Many of these imagined futures are also somewhat dystopian. Which, as we are surrounded by the angry worlds of Twitter and Facebook and the superficial imagery of Instagram is not that surprising! Despite our belief in the unique situation of our times history also tells us that it has always been thus. Piranesi, a Roman engraver of the C18th, imagined a dense classical dystopia whose plays of perception and perspective have echoed through time to Escher onto Fritz Lang and into our virtual world of games.

I suggest that this dystopian tendency is because each generation, as it ages, looks back fondly to their own rosy infancy. Which is not that surprising as the past offers a happier prospect than the inevitability of 'shuffling off this mortal coil'.

I am an architect and thus an optimist. Indeed it is my professional condition to help the collective vision move from the darkness of shuffling off coils towards the shimmering joys of sunlit uplands! And with the world facing the existential challenge of climate change never has this been more vital.

So my Town of the Future is bathed in the variable delights of seasonal sunshine. Shadow and reflection mark out the streets and squares unfettered by the pallid gloom of a once polluted sky. Vegetation rich in colour offers shade and shelter for all. For our town is very much part urban forest part urban allotment both at ground level and at roof level. Indeed no surface is wasted as food is grown everywhere and sold locally. This urban Wilding has served both to transform our old town and to allow the countryside around to return to a nitrate free pre C20th condition where the ever greater ecosystem of plants, animals and insects flourish.

The quiet of our town's transport systems of trains, trams, bikes and silent cars means we can hear the buzz of the wildlife in our daily promenades. Which means we all walk ever more as we travel from home to work to school and everywhere in between. And the inbetween is ever more lively with people growing, making, selling and repairing roof, goods, services and life's essential luxuries.

It is wonderful to see our old town coming back to life. Once dead high streets are busy again at ground and above as the old homes are restored and new ones extend two, three, four more stories into the sky. We live in a multi layered town where distinct neighbourhoods of very different spatial and architectural character flourish side by side. People work, live and play side by side and there is a general acceptance of the need to 'rub along' for the greater good.

Indeed it is the greater good that has defined our town. We talk more and text less. We recycle materials and food just as we do buildings and goods. We have more time to enjoy ourselves: to read; to think; to learn and to come together to work and to play. Life has slowed down but we actually produce more - which was vital on our journey to this delightful town we have collectively reinvented. It has allowed the sharing of happiness and also given us more time to travel and connect with the wider world in person. To learn from other places, from other towns.

At a glimpse, our town looks very much as it did fifty years ago at the turn of the last Millennium. And on further inspection it looks ever more like it did in the pre Victorian era before the onslaught of fossil fuels, industrialisation and then the motorcar. Of course it has been endlessly adapted, extended and reinvented and it is that very layering of history, the mark of each generation, that makes it our town

---

SIMON ALLFORD is a founding Director of AHMM where he leads a design studio of two hundred architects. He is a frequent writer, critic, judge and advisor; a visiting professor at Harvard; a previous chairman of the Architecture Foundation; and currently a trustee of the London School of Architecture and the Chickenshed Theatres Trust. He is also President of the Royal Institute of British Architects.

**ALLFORD
HALL
MONAGHAN
MORRIS**

Established in 1989, ALLFORD HALL MONAGHAN MORRIS makes buildings that are satisfying and enjoyable to use, beautiful to look at and easy to understand. Winner of the RIBA Stirling Prize in 2015 and many other awards for architecture and design, AHMM has received public, client and media acclaim for its work on education, commercial, residential, arts and masterplanning projects around the UK, the US and internationally.

KATIE BALDERSON

The Portman Estate

T he "Town of the Future" will be a destination which improves the quality of life for all those who live, work and visit. It must do this while delivering cleaner, greener and healthier ways of living. This is the wish of all of us who work in the built environment. To achieve this ambition we need to be open to new ideas and innovation. We also need to challenge existing models of urban living.

Our towns and cities are already experiencing the impact of climate change. Changing weather patterns are making many of our buildings unbearably hot in the summer months and at greater risk of flooding during severe rainfall. We also know that our buildings are responsible for a significant amount of our carbon emissions, but if we can find ways to reduce the carbon footprint of our built environment, we have the opportunity to make a lasting impact. The scale of the challenge is huge, but so is the opportunity. We need designers, innovators and activists to seize the challenge.

Firstly, The Town of the Future will need buildings which are designed as flexible spaces for a mix of uses and users. As occupiers come and go, buildings will need to adapt to changing requirements but be built to last. For many years we thought that our commercial buildings had a natural lifecycle: at the end of its life a building would be demolished to make way for something bigger and more contemporary. This is no longer the default position as we seek more sustainable ways to regenerate workplaces.

Designing a flexible building with a longer lifecycle requires a shift in approach. Typically, the older buildings in our towns are our heritage buildings, protected from development due to their architectural or historic significance. The buildings in The

Town of the Future may well be many of the ones we see today, but reimagined and retrofitted with flexibility, diversity and sustainability at their heart.

Secondly, in The Town of the Future there will be greater significance on the spaces between buildings: the pavements, roads and public areas. Designers will need to find clever ways to introduce more green spaces amongst buildings. These spaces will provide areas of refuge for people and wildlife. They should help with the impact of climate change by providing shade, drainage and urban biodiversity. Good design of these public areas significantly improves quality of life, and in The Town of the Future these in-between spaces will be as important as the buildings themselves.

Finally, The Town of the Future will be less dominated by private cars. The rising cost and environmental impact of owning your own car will reach a tipping point. For journeys where public transport is not practical then car sharing, renting and gig economy schemes will be increasingly popular. The storage of cars on streets will decrease, creating opportunities for new in-between spaces. In The Town of the Future, our urban and traffic designers will need to adapt to this new model, providing safe, accessible streets for electric bicycles, automated deliveries, car pools and perhaps more walking!

As we move towards The Town of the Future we will need skill, energy and determination to make the transition to a more sustainable way of living. Much can be achieved through good urban management which supports happy and healthy communities. It is an exciting time to be working in this sector and to have the opportunity to contribute towards these significant and lasting changes.

KATIE BALDERSON joined The Portman Estate in 2009 as Estate Secretary. In 2020 she was appointed to the Board as Corporate Director, a role which covers all aspects of governance, compliance and business support. Katie also manages the Estate's sustainability programme including various environmental and charitable initiatives.

THE PORTMAN ESTATE is situated in the heart of central London, just north of Hyde Park. Covering 110 acres of Marylebone, the Estate has been in the ownership of the Portman family for nearly 500 years. It offers a vibrant mix of commercial, retail and residential space and is home to a welcoming and diverse community. Over recent years we have worked especially hard to restore many Georgian buildings to today's high standards and create contemporary homes and offices that reflect their historical context. We have also launched a number of new, mixed-use developments which have attracted a wide range of occupiers including independent retailers, award-winning restaurants and boutique hotels.

CHRIS DE PURY
& ZAHRA BARDAI

Bryan Cave Leighton Paisner LLP

The Town of the Future will be sustainably constructed, co-existing with the natural environment by replenishing those resources which it takes and designed in a way which breaks down the societal barriers to inequality. Or perhaps that should read The Town of the Future should? There is no doubt that if we were to sit down with a blank sheet of paper and sketch out what our future towns and cities should look like it is not difficult to imagine how this kind of utopia could be achieved. A town designed with basic entitlements at its heart around which the physical environment is evolved. Healthcare, education, employment opportunities, recreational activity and improved physical and mental wellbeing freely accessible to all. A town with an infrastructure which ensures equal and continuous access to fundamental human entitlements such as food, clean water and shelter, sanitation and security. All of this created in a manner which reflects the impact we have on our surroundings, each other and the planet. None of this is particularly novel.

And what does this utopia look like? The possibilities are endless. Certainly if we were to start from scratch it would make sense to mandate that all component elements of the physical environment are biodegradable or at the very least recyclable, offsetting the resultant carbon impact. Every element of every building will be utilised in order to give back what it takes from the natural environment. Indeed new materials and building operating systems are already starting to do this and new technology is being developed all the time such as glazing which doubles up as a solar cell. Green energy is of course key but cities and towns will need to also create as much energy as they use. In fact, The Town of the Future will need to be as self-sufficient as it can be utilising all available space to generate resources such as roof top and underground farming. Smart city technology is "in built" in the same way as traditional utilities. Towns and cities are capable of harnessing big data which is used in order to improve society including seamlessly linking transport systems and connectivity to all areas removing segregation and other barriers to equal opportunity. Public transport will be key to making this work but it has to be safer, affordable and efficient. There are some cities experimenting with this now such as Miami which is contemplating the use of a personal rapid transport system. Citizens of these towns will have proximity and accessibility to facilities including schools, hospitals and facilities for the elderly and infirm rather than facilities being far flung or in less desirable locations. The concept of "urban hubs" have been mooted as the solution and instead of one city centre there may be multiple localised communities containing everything the residents could need so reducing their carbon footprint and fostering better integration between different cultures and ages. This kind of community living has positive impacts for law and order reducing the need for formal intervention.

Again many of these concepts and the technology which complements them is not new and either exists or is within the realms of the possible. So why is progress so slow? One important question to ask in answering this is whether it is possible to mould our existing towns and cities to create the ideal Town of the Future? Certainly cities such as Singapore and Copenhagen have made significant inroads. The investment required to create the ideal Town of the Future is significant. Razing our cities and towns to the ground is certainly not imaginable right now. There is no question that events such as COP22 and activists and environmentalists, including Greta Thunberg and David Attenborough, have demonstrated the need and commitment to achieving net zero by 2050. This is only possible by grafting new technology onto the existing physical environment and replacing what currently exists as and when possible. But the utopian Town of the Future could be so much more than this. Perhaps then the physical, tangible Town of the Future won't in fact actually look that different. Perhaps the utopian Town of the Future we envisage can only be achieved to its full potential in the meta verse where it can be developed from the grass roots up? Perhaps The Town of the Future is a hybrid? As CS Lewis said, "You can't go back and change the beginning, but you can start where you are and change the ending."

BCLP's Global Head of Real Estate CHRIS DE PURY specialises in complex and multi-faceted real estate transactions including structured investments and disposals, joint ventures and developments of both single asset and portfolios. He has been rated in the top tier of real estate lawyers for over 20 years (Chambers and Partners), Hall of Fame (The Legal 500), three times included in the Hot 100 most influential lawyers (The Lawyer), one of only two lawyers nominated for their business acumen (Global Lawyers) and most recently was nominated by peers as Real Estate lawyer of the year (London) (Best Lawyers in UK). "Chris de Pury is a class act...a quality operator. The number one real estate lawyer in the country." *Chambers and Partners, 2021.*

ZAHRA BARDAI is Global Chief Operating Officer – Real Estate at BCLP. Prior to becoming global COO for the market leading real estate team at BCLP, Zahra spent over 10 years as a commercial real estate lawyer, advising on a broad range of transactions including structured disposals and acquisitions utilising a variety of tax efficient vehicles, joint ventures, and real estate aspects of property finance (acting for both borrower and lender). As COO she is responsible for the international operations of the team, working across the legal, finance and business support teams to drive forward the real estate strategy.

With over 1,400 lawyers in 30 offices across North America, Europe, the Middle East and Asia, BRYAN CAVE LEIGHTON PAISNER LLP is a fully integrated global law firm that provides clients with connected legal advice, wherever and whenever they need it. Our global team of nearly 700 real estate sector lawyers represents clients in acquiring, developing, financing, leasing, operating, managing and selling commercial real estate covering all major asset classes.

TAMI CHUANG

Heimstaden

The Town of the Future will... reflect the values that we as a society choose to embrace. It can look like a big metropolis, dense, full of people who mingle and mesh, living a shared experience. Or we can live in compartmentalised, digital lives where human interaction is mediated by devices and kept virtual as much as possible. It can look like a quaint village, where we cohabit with a chosen few – our family, friends or will it be only people with whom we share the same beliefs?

We have ventured down many paths of town building in the past. We made rules, separated uses, zoned our way to a health and safety utopia, or so we thought. Originally we grew organically, adding spaces as needed – a shop, a shed, a secondary dwelling to house family nearby. We have settled near water we used to irrigate; we have built around ports so we can navigate. We have towns where people lived in a communal way, as well as towns assembled to house the industrial labourers. We thought technology could liberate us, untether us from cities, their offices, traffic and pollution - where in fact we can be dispersed in far flung corners of the world. Recently we realised that we are rather social beings because we like to be near people who make us happy, who inspire us and support us.

The Town of the Future will reflect the values that we as a society hold dear. I heard this from a teacher years ago. It struck me as an idealistic vision or something like a metaphor not to be taken literally. Over the years I saw how this 'Town of the Future' changed as we ourselves have, with growing ambitions, aspirations, and at times reservations. In many places people became fatigued by our dependence on cars, and so fostered a compact town where one can walk around to fulfil many of the daily needs or utilised alternative modes of transport. In other places people sought security, and built a fortress to protect themselves, where different people did not have to mix, living parallel lives that bore little resemblance. How we see ourselves relating to the community around us manifested physically in the way our surroundings are built. It gets codified in planning laws and transportation policies. It enforces our beliefs. It feels right. Or does it?

We learn from trial and error, what works and what doesn't. The way we judge this often depends on what is happening in the world, and it's often through backward looking lenses. At times we feel confident while at other times we feel scared. This is reflected in how we build our homes, our cities, our countries. So what will The Town of the Future look like? It will depend on the values that we as a collective embrace, and chose to live by.

———————————

TAMI CHUANG is an experienced real estate investment management professional with extensive experience spanning indirect investing, fund formation, capital raising, investor relations, business development, and urban design. Currently based in London, she has 15 years of experience in the fund management industry and enjoys working with global institutions to develop solutions to meet their real estate investment objectives. Tami has a Master in City Planning from MIT and a MBA from Columbia Business School in the City of New York.

Heimstaden
Friendly Homes

HEIMSTADEN is a leading owner, manager, and operator of rental housing across 10 European countries, representing 150,000 units and over €30B in GAV. At Heimstaden, we enrich and simplify life through friendly homes. This is the vision which drives, motivates and inspires us along with our corporate values to Care, Dare, and Share. We care and want to make a positive difference in the lives of our employees, customers, partners and the society we live in. We dare to come up with ideas that are new, diverse and unexpected. We share our knowledge, expertise and experience. Get to know us better at: corporate.heimstaden.com/home/default.aspx

MARC GILBARD

Moorfield Group

The Town of the Future will reflect not only the demographic, commercial and social trends that are current at that time, but also those in the process of evolving and emerging. However, 'path dependency' will remain relevant as the past matters in ways which are not necessarily helpful in the present i.e. The Town of the Future will come with baggage!

Housing will be challenged by a growing population wanting to live in an environmentally and socially acceptable way and no matter how much society changes and technology develops to tackle issues such as energy, waste and carbon emissions, there are going to be significant hurdles individually and collectively to achieve this, considering the starting point. Development of new housing, alongside refurbishment and improvement of existing housing stock will have materially tighter regulations to adhere to, if there is any chance of meeting the climate change goals that will allow those living in the future to enjoy the planet in similar ways to those in the past.

The ongoing acceptance and embracing of more flexible working will result in The

Town of the Future having satellite and shared workplaces close to the employee's residential accommodation as well as the living accommodation itself also fulfilling the desire of the employee to work from home. This will not take away from the need for a central headquarters office for many organisations, but it does mean smaller, more inviting city centre offices. The era of the tripartite working environment will have fully emerged!

Whether for reasons of environmental impact, noise pollution or safety, The Town of the Future will not permit privately owned vehicles within an inner perimeter. Transport will be through environmentally acceptable means or by enhanced and appropriate public transport modes. Driverless taxis, intra-town buses and trams and inter-town trains running along relevant designated routes will complement the materially greater pedestrianised streets and the multiple private transport pathways. Commercial vehicles will deliver their stock into future towns overnight and within limited permitted times to reduce congestion and disruption – and where possible alternative routes for deliveries will be found, whether under or over ground, thereby making the supply chain more efficient. Most people will rent cars for their journeys outside of town centres leading to strategically located open storage sites for hire cars on the fringes of the town centres.

The rise of online consumer gratification will continue, and physical retail stores will form a central hub within every future town. The retail will be anchored by leisure provision to increase dwell times and encourage individuals, groups and families to congregate and socialise. The retail that was once sitting on the spokes leading away from the hub will become housing resulting in many social and environmental benefits for the town.

Each Town of the Future will have their own schools for the young, care for the old and primary and secondary care for the sick. Towns will have their own emergency services that take care of their community and which will be held to account by those they serve. Politics will be more local and less national with a better end result for the Country as a whole. These local keyworkers will live in the town and will be recognised for the essential work they do and so rewarded accordingly.

Towns will work to develop a personality of their own rather than the homogenous approach of the recent past. This will result in greater tourism between towns, and from outside the Country, as people explore the past and future offered by each unique location. Hotels and other forms of short stay accommodation will also differentiate themselves to become a leisure experience in their own right rather than simply a place to rest overnight.

Social awareness will become a dominant force within all towns of the future, allowing the local population and visitors to enjoy their life experiences without the disruptive antisocial behaviour of others. As such, schooling, policing, community care, leisure, entertainment and many other social drivers will reflect the need for cooperative social empathy. Full gainful employment in the future town will be pursued through a benefits system that encourages a 'community workforce' so that everyone who is able to work has a purpose and contributes to the wellbeing of all, no matter the task.

Finally, every Town of the Future will offer multiple options of locally produced food and drink. Surrounding the town will be farmland that reflects and promotes healthy free-range live-stock and a greater demand for seasonal fruit and vegetables. Local industry will also return and although many supply chains will remain global there will be a much greater emphasis on locally produced goods and services, thereby boosting the future towns' economic growth and employment whilst materially reducing their collective carbon footprint.

———

MARC GILBARD has been the CEO of Moorfield since 1996 and has led Moorfield's transformation from a small company listed on the London Stock Exchange into one of the leading UK real estate private equity fund managers. Marc initially specialised in investment and development finance and then became a top-rated real estate equity analyst and advisor prior to becoming a private equity investor. In October 2011, the Howard de Walden Estate appointed Marc to its Board as a Non-Executive Director, he now Chairs the Investment Committee and serves on the Audit Committee. In April 2016 Marc became Chairman of Audley Retirement Villages and a member of their Investment Committee. Marc has advised as a Policy Committee Member of the British Property Federation (BPF), a Member of the Property Advisory Group to the Bank of England, a Member of the Investment Property Forum (IPF) and a Member of the Royal Institution of Chartered Surveyors (RICS).

MOORFIELD GROUP is a leading UK real estate fund manager with a 26-year track record of investing across most sectors of UK Real Estate. Moorfield is especially well known as a vanguard investor in emerging operational real estate sectors. Moorfield operates under a proven investment and asset management structure which enables it to be a vertically integrated (in-house) asset manager, and also to partner with groups that have specialist operational or development expertise. Moorfield's own expertise uniquely positions it to appraise risk and deliver attractive returns to investors, while ensuring that it strives to meet the highest ESG standards. Since 2005 Moorfield has raised six real estate funds; five Moorfield Real Estate Funds (MREFs) together with a dedicated senior housing platform, Moorfield Audley Real Estate Fund.

DARSHITA GILLIES

Maanch

The Town of the Future will be SUBSCRIBED!

The Subscription Economy is a landscape in which the traditional pay-per-product (or service) models are moving towards subscription-based pay-per-month (or year) models.

In the context of a Town, different bundles of services, facilities, resources will be able to be bought as a unit per month or annually.

To flesh this out a bit more, imagine it is 2050, Jane Doe has just completed university and has landed her first job at a leading multinational company. Her job requires her to travel frequently across continents and work with different teams. Instead of having a base in London her hometown and traveling in and out of London to visit other office locations, Jane has decided to subscribe to the 'Platinum Package' of TownX.

SO, WHAT IS TOWNX?

TownX is a growing group of global Towns where high-performing, eco-conscious, fun-loving communities live in and out of. TownX exists in every country, and has every aspect of your living embedded to encompass an integrated offering to keep you at your best—all the time, any time. The towns within the TownX Group have a "circular strategy" which combines the principles of a "circular economy" to reduce, reuse and recycle materials across consumer goods, building materials and food. Regional policies within each town aim to protect the environment and natural resources, reduce social exclusion and guarantee good living standards for all.

Jane currently lives in TownX-Mayfair. She wakes up in her comfy minimalist 1 bedroom room and goes to the gym - She doesn't pay a separate membership fee for the gym. After a steam and shower she walks to the cafe nearby for a healthy breakfast and a sustainably sourced coffee - she doesn't pay for it either. She then gets in a self-drive car to head to her office - no payment or pre-booking or parking permit needed. She works till noon and chooses a nearby restaurant for lunch (no pay needed) and gets back to work. Her evenings she spends on hobbies or going out with friends or simply streaming entertainment home. She didn't use her wallet the entire day. She doesn't pay monthly rent, nor do electricity, telecom and water bills concern her.

That's because subscribing to a package of TownX gives her access to all the products and services allocated to the package. Living in TownX also appeals to Jane as she can easily move from TownX-Mayfair to TownX-Mumbai or to TownX-Mombasa and get a similar bundle of products and services allocated to her.

SO, WHY ARE TOWNX SUBSCRIPTIONS RISING?

TownX packages are flexible and can be upgraded and down-sized based on the evolving needs of the subscribers. Unused products/services get reallocated to them as credits and overused ones get charged pro-rata.

All individuals subscribed to the TownX model know that it is more economical, sustainable, enjoyable and hassle-free for them.

All entities serving within the TownX ecosystem are networked and purpose-driven and one of their primary objectives is to optimize resource production and consumption. Many of these entities were large conglomerates that saw the opportunity in becoming part of a collaborative venture that enabled them to break silos and deliver efficiencies at scale. Unlimited growth is not their goal, their goal is to serve quality products/services to their stakeholders.

The governance within TownX is transparent and power is distributed.

Inhabitants of TownX explore and enjoy their life and when in face of challenge they come together to innovate and find solutions.

HOW DID TOWNX COME TO BE?

IPCC (Intergovernmental Panel on Climate Change) had unequivocally confirmed that human influence had warmed the atmosphere, ocean and land and human impact on the climate system was clear and growing, to the extent that we were consuming the very foundations of our existence at a rate faster than the planet could replenish.

The base architecture to get us into a sustainable state was laid out within the Sustainable Development Goals (SDG's) framework at the end of 2015. 17 action-oriented universally applicable goals to address various issues, including ending poverty and hunger, improving health and education, making cities more sustainable, combating climate change, and protecting oceans and forests etc. were agreed and accepted by 192 countries.

Several micro and macro innovations and purpose-led entrepreneurship led to the several iterations until the current TownX model came to be.

Many believe that the TownX model is constantly being refined as new innovations and new information become part of its ever maturing natural intelligence.

Listed among 2021 ESG & Diversity Trailblazer - Modern Governance 100 by Diligent, 100 Most Meaningful Business Leader 2020 and 100 Most Influential in UK-India Relations, DARSHITA GILLIES is Founder & CEO of Maanch - a multi-award winning global impact management systems for investors, corporates and the philanthropy ecosystem.

Launched in 2018, MAANCH works with 700+ partners across 30+ countries to achieve the UN-SDGs. A Chartered Accountant, Investment Banker, Executive Coach and FinTech-Blockchain Specialist, ESG & Impact Evangelist, Darshita serves on the Boards of a few For-Profit and Non-Profit organisations. She is known for her inclusive leadership, and innovative approach to solving systemic challenges.

JIM GOTT
& LEE ROBINS

Mount Street

The Town of the Future will… look very similar to current towns, however, if you look closely you will see some significant changes.

To begin with, towns are not sprawling, they are well planned, mid-sized and are designed with functionality and community as the key aims. This has allowed all amenities to be accessible within a short travel window and has in turn facilitated the use of sustainable transport. It has also resulted in the provision of better amenities and a greater sense of community.

More efficient use of energy resources and reduction in carbon emissions is wide ranging, but is also one of the least obvious changes. Buildings are constructed using advanced low-carbon materials and carbon sequestering materials and many buildings have been 'recycled' to reuse the existing carbon encapsulating structure and couple it with energy efficient refurbishments. The buildings themselves are energy efficient and equipped with smart technologies. Buildings incorporate localised power generation and direct air capture systems that remove CO_2 from the atmosphere. This coupled with large-scale, edge of town power generation and district heating systems allow us to enjoy our low carbon environment.

In the suburbs, the design of single dwelling housing has become more efficient. The increase in buildings costs has been offset by a reduction in living space, with buildings being designed for efficient use. The use of organic, carbon offset materials such as timber, is notable in low-rise development.

As towns have developed, greater integration of rich and poor has resulted in the integration of all housing types in all locations. This integration of communities has had wide ranging positive effects in terms of improved levels of education and employment and a reduction in crime.

Evidence of climate change impact can also be seen. Building resilience is evident in some areas as the effects of climate change have been marked by increased flooding, water scarcity and days of excessive heat. The impact of climate change can also be seen in our agricultural processes, and has created a requirement for large vertical farms to be present in towns, providing locally produced vegetables all year round.

Much of the smart technology relates to building automation and efficiency as well allowing companies to monitor the efficient use of buildings. The smart technology also integrates with the wider smart town technology, allowing users to determine how the town is being used and to target resources, such as transport.

The use of the buildings in the town centre has changed too, it is notable that many areas that would have been retail sites have transitioned to leisure, to help create vibrant town centres which encourage residents to interact.

In general, industrial and heavy commercial businesses have been centralised to edge of town locations. This aids with transport provision and allows businesses to interact with one another and share benefits and processes. Waste heat schemes are present at these locations taking the heat generated from industrial processes, storing it, and delivering it to residential properties via district heating schemes.

Flexible working has created a demand for serviced offices, but traditional offices have also followed this model. Hot desking is now entirely normal, flexible working hours are normal and offices include a lot more space for collaborative working.

Schools, colleges, hospitals, and similar buildings are no longer value engineered, instead they are designed to achieve the best results and to have long lifespans. This has resulted in both better facilities and lower operating costs.

Transport in The Town of the Future is very different; cycles and scooters become mainstream and use the roads that are no longer accessible to cars. Secure storage and charge stations are present throughout the town and at many offices and public buildings. Public transport is all electric and, along with the self-driving electric taxis, is the only way to access the town centre. The low cost of the electric self-driving taxis has negated the need for car ownership in towns, which has removed the need for much on street and off-street parking.

The design of the town has also changed, with residential and business areas co-located, such that amenities are located within walking distance of people's houses. This has shown benefits in terms of access to amenities as well as having fostered a greater sense of community.

The future town described here though is perhaps not so far off. Our towns are evolving around us with some of these new technologies already introduced, and the way we design buildings and plan towns is already accepted as good practice by some. By their very nature as a collection of fixed in place buildings and infrastructure, our towns are often slow and expensive to change. Compared to the rapid advancements in medical science or space travel, the often subtle and slow changes to our towns may look rather mundane. Rest assured though, change is coming, in fact it's never stopped. It's just going to take a while that's all.

JIM GOTT has over 25 years' experience in the real estate, engineering, environmental and power and energy markets and has worked at senior level on hundreds of projects in the UK and throughout Europe.

Over the last ten years Jim has managed hundreds of CRE debt and equity projects amounting to many billions of £s / €s / $s of loans, acquisitions and divestitures.

LEE ROBINS has a strong background in commercial real estate banking and asset management with Pan-European and UK experience across all asset classes. He has managed large and complex real estate loans and equity co-investments and has extensive experience in restructuring distressed debt positions, underwriting, deal sourcing and investment, consultancy and development. Lee holds a MASc (Banking and Finance) and BASc (Property & Economics).

MOUNTSTREET

MOUNT STREET is a leading solutions provider to the investment community, delivering tailored products to investors and lenders participating in a full range of credit markets. We provide services across the front, middle and back office to our clients throughout the loan lifecycle, with market leading expertise, a trusted team of professionals and a proprietary technology system driving service excellence.

Mount Street is an independent business which has grown rapidly since being founded in 2013 and now has a global footprint that enables us to offer an unparalleled service to our clients. Our comprehensive product offering extends throughout the lifecycle of our clients' activities: from providing origination and due diligence services through outsourced loan administration and facility agency to portfolio management and investment management services. Those services are provided across the full range of credit products, from real estate and other asset backed lending to structured finance markets. We currently service clients from offices in Europe, the US and Australia and we continue to grow. At Mount Street, we pride ourselves on meeting our clients' needs by developing leading edge technology, innovating with an entrepreneurial approach and delivering through a culture of excellence. Our vision is to provide a complete ecosystem of outsourced solutions for the credit investment sector.

PETER HAYES

PGIM Real Estate

The Town of the Future will in thirty years be known for how connected it is – both with itself and with the world. This will be about virtual connectivity but also physical. No matter the technological breakthroughs, at its heart, The Town of the Future is about community – that people will still want (and need) to be together. To the eye the connectivity of this town will be most apparent through technological advances in transit and travel. Breakthroughs in cold fusion and natural energy capture reduce energy costs significantly accelerating changes. For one is the prevalence of various automated transport systems. Time to wait, time to travel and cost still matter though which means options to "pick-up" or "collect" also matter. But it is all to hand – no matter where you are in the town. Disaggregated storage systems increase accessibility as do the sheer speed in which cars and bikes and scooters travel. Wait time is minimal.

The speed of travel wouldn't be possible without it being controlled and managed. Self-driving vehicles are governed by onboard, street and satellite guidance systems – linked to town traffic management systems. But the limitations of AI means auto travel is only permitted where manual travel is banned. Very few people now own cars.

The organization of travel means technological advances have helped in overcoming simple geography. Time is now the measure of distance not miles. And that allows The Town of the Future to spread giving people far more choice as to where they need to live. People can be both further away and yet feel close by. The impact of this spread means land prices even out. Concerns about having to physically live near good schools, near emergency services, near relatives, near work are diminished.

Innovations in homes also helps make people feel connected. Aside from the rise of 'near-actual' meetings, get togethers, training sessions and so on, as well as "living in the metaverse", all from the comfort of the home, options exist for "ever present" real time connectivity with friends and neighbours (including emergency services). These all help manage concerns about health and well-being, as well as security. But automatic home management systems (that can be overridden) do not stop there – from dealing with utility providers (notably water and waste) to the grocery store – repetitive, manual tasks are being replaced. Autobots are everywhere.

What is equally impressive are the innovations in building and design – significantly reducing the environmental costs of construction. The big part being played here is the evolution of semi organic-synthetic materials and how they incorporate energy capture and storage capabilities – notably solar energy. Self-repairing technology (along with self-cleaning clothes) is coming but is not here yet.

These innovations in construction are apparent in all new buildings in and around the town – but also around irrigation and water management that has given rise to in-town vertical farms. The use of moisture extraction as well as plant food technology has seen a proliferation in farms over the last 10 years – locally grown produce takes on a whole new meaning!

Town centres will not have changed that much over the past 30 years. Green spaces are far more prevalent – thanks to light directing technology in building designs – as is the wider pedestrianization of the centre. Much of which is welcomed by the health and well-being lobby.

Shops still exist, and not just those selling a service but those selling goods and a service. From green grocers to book stores. Although you can know their stock inventory before you visit, particular goods and services are only available in person. Aside from being offered personal deals as you wander in (based off existing buying patterns), you can also get tailored nutritional advice and fashion tips. Staff have become more skilled.

The upskilling of all jobs is why places of work – such as the office – still exist. Homeworking is prevalent but the number of jobs in the creative/knowledge base has grown as automation continues to replace repetitive tasks. Problem solving, innovation solutions, new product ideas and so on have grown in importance and are achieved better through in person meetings. Innovations from sound wave manipulation (alongside voice recognition software) and movable fixtures and fittings for example also helps – giving workers choices/control over their environment.

Office buildings cluster as their physical proximity generates benefits for businesses. This ranges from shared experiences to shared information that the virtual world still cannot beat. But this is also why town living remains popular. Here apartments and houses offer people a physical link to home, work and play. That is back to how connected it is. The biggest congregation of amenities, of services, of shops, alongside places to work and live is still in and around The Town of the Future.

PETER HAYES is a managing director at PGIM Real Estate and global head of Investment Research. Based in London, Peter is responsible for overseeing a global team that provides strategic advice and support to the investment management divisions of the business. Peter is a member of the Global and European Investment Committees and the Global Product Committee. Prior to joining PGIM Real Estate in 2007, Peter held a number of positions, including director and global head of economic and real estate forecasting for DTZ, an international property advisory company; UK economist at the Bank of England; and lecturer in economics at the Universities of Sheffield and King's College London.

Peter has a bachelor's degree in economics from University College, Swansea, a master's degree in macroeconomics from the University of Liverpool, and a doctorate in applied economics from the University of Sheffield.

As one of the largest real estate managers in the world with US$209.3 billion in gross assets under management and administration,[1] **PGIM REAL ESTATE** strives to deliver exceptional outcomes for investors and borrowers through a range of real estate equity and debt solutions across the risk-return spectrum. PGIM Real Estate is a business of PGIM, the US$1.5 trillion global asset management business of Prudential Financial, Inc. (NYSE: PRU). PGIM Real Estate's rigorous risk management, seamless execution, and extensive industry insights are backed by a 50-year legacy of investing in commercial real estate, a 140-year history of real estate financing,[2] and the deep local expertise of over 1,100 professionals in 32 cities globally. Through its investment, financing, asset management, and talent management approach, PGIM Real Estate engages in practices that ignite positive environmental and social impact, while pursuing activities that strengthen communities around the world. For more information visit pgimrealestate.com.

---

[1]   As of December 31, 2021, AUM reflected as gross. Net AUM is $137.9B and AUA is $45.9B

[2]   Includes legacy lending through PGIM's parent company, Prudential Financial, Inc

CHRIS KANE

O'Shea Group

BRITAIN'S TOWNS IN THE 21ST-CENTURY – A RENAISSANCE OPPORTUNITY

The best route forward for British towns of the future is to go back to their roots. Since over the last 60/70 years British towns have somewhat lost their way and have been blighted by a cocktail of poor urban planning, a misguided love affair with the car and a fixation with department stores and retail chains, compounded by the explosion of commuting. The magnetic effect of the bigger city has caused many places to become little more than dormitory towns, devoid of life during the working week.

In recent years much has been written about the demise of British towns. According to John Carvell[1] "Britain's town centres are rapidly becoming indistinguishable losing all sense of local identity". This was reaffirmed by a NEF[2] report which concludes that, "the nation's high streets have been taken over by a phenomenon – **clone town Britain**". All of which have given rise to see calls for fresh thinking including the Grimsey review which asked: ***"Is it time to reshape our town centres?"*** As we look forward to 2022 has this time arrived, at long last?

One of the unintended consequences of Covid-19 is that we might see a reversal and possibly a return to a time when towns had character, charm and commerce. As opposed to the bland blend of multiples, charity shops and vacant spaces in the centre, surrounded by soulless housing estates, patchy public services and car dependent out-of-town retail stores.

As with the period following the Black Death in the Middle Ages, are we now entering a period of renaissance? For the first time ever the entire world is changing in tandem. We are beginning to realise that there is no going back to life as we knew it and the implications of change are still emerging but they are significant. One likely example is the death of commuting on a regular basis. Accompanied by the end of the standard "Monday to Friday, 9-to-5" working week. With such upheavals in the pipeline, there is even more reason to take inspiration from Leonardo da Vinci who noted that we must ***"Learn how to see. Realise that everything connects to everything else"***.

1   www.theguardian.com/uk/2005/jun/06/money.shopping

2   neweconomics.org/uploads/files/1da089b4b1e66ba2b3_v8m6b0c0w.pdf

Along with all its negative aspects, Covid-19 has unleashed an enormous societal shift. In my mind this provides a tremendous opportunity to reinvent our towns, to apply renaissance thinking and to start a journey towards a more human centric approach to urban living. In terms of Britain's towns coming out of lockdown whilst learning to live with pandemic times. This offers us the chance to reflect on the evolution of the town, its fundamental purpose, its people and activity orientation and how various functions interconnect with each other – in other words, to go back to our roots

We now need as a nation to get to grips with the situation and adopt a renaissance spirit to the problem. Here are six key areas of focus which should help us get to grips with the situation and if implemented in unison should generate positive outcomes:

1. **Refocus the High Street** on traditional mixed use, including public & health services.
2. **Increase active curation** of town centres on a year-round basis, it's not just streetscapes but how they are operated and enlivened.
3. **Reassess the role of the car and public transport**, stand back and take a fresh look at how people and goods move around an urban area.
4. **Get serious about the climate change imperative**, prioritise the green/biophilia dimension when making decisions especially when considering refurbishment activities.
5. **Strengthen urban leadership**, empower local government to take a longer-term perspective rather than one governed by politics. Build effective partnerships with citizens and stakeholders.
6. **Be bolder with decision making** - inject more imagination into the reshaping process, actively seek the views of the leaders of the future and purposefully engage with people who actually live in our towns and consume its amenities.

These ingredients should help towns to break out from the narrow frame of reference of recent decades and its accompanying negativity. We need to rethink our urban planning methods and base them on the principle of people and place, not the other way around. We need to reimagine how towns work based on their original purpose and reframe the purpose of our town centres

Whilst one must recognise that change is always difficult, it is fraught with difficulty and hampered by inertia brought about by vested interests. Now is the time to strike out and be bold! In doing so we could take as a guiding principle some advice from the inventor of the polio vaccine Dr Jonas Salk – **our greatest responsibility is to be good ancestors**.

CHRIS KANE has worked in the Corporate Real Estate sector for over 30 years, having operated as the Vice President of International Corporate Real Estate for The Walt Disney Company, before acting as Head of Corporate Real Estate at the BBC, where he was responsible for the creation of MediaCityUK in Salford and oversaw the £1bn development of Broadcasting House.

He is a Fellow of the Royal Institution of Chartered Surveyors and a founding member and director of Six Ideas, a global consultancy focused on workplace development and innovation. He sits on the editorial board of the *Corporate Real Estate Journal*, and is also a regular contributor to the *LEADER* magazine.

Founded in 1966, O'SHEA GROUP has over 55 years' experience in construction and development. Starting out as a concrete frame contractor, today it is uniquely positioned as a residential-led investor, developer and main contractor currently involved in over £2 billion of development in the UK.

Covering the living and commercial sectors for both public and private clients, O'Shea's private ownership and experienced management team gives it flexibility to acquire opportunities and subsequently build out the developments. O'Shea's vision for long term success is centred around partnership with its supply chain, development partners, and funders alike - many it has worked with for over 25 years. A four-year running Top Track 250 company, O'Shea continues to grow while boasting industry beating profitability and balance sheet strength.

AUDREY KLEIN

Planet Smart City

THE CITY AND COMMUNITY "OF THE FUTURE" EXISTS TODAY!

Planet Smart City has created a new category of technologically enabled affordable housing community which also has an Impact Strategy and ESG Goals. Planet delivers positive social impact by developing environmentally, economically and socially conscious communities. Planet's purpose is to tackle the global deficit in affordable housing and give more people access to high-quality infrastructure, smart homes, technology and shared services so that they can build sustainable communities.

Planet professionals and community managers stay on site long after construction work has finished and oversee education programmes and digital services for residents to build thriving communities that people are proud to call home.

Global corporate sponsors (such as Swiss Re) help Planet fulfil this mission; for example, through educating communities on personal finance and providing basic financial products. Such partnerships generate tangible mutual benefits; for example, "smart" smoke alarms installed by Planet de-risk fire insurance for the communities re-insured by Swiss Re. Other ways that Planet offers better quality of life to its residents through its partnerships:

- Volunteer mentors help residents build financial goals and track record
- Co-creation with Planet of digital offering to gamify financial tips
- Personalized home/life insurance offers affordable for Planet residents

Planet's impact strategy is aligned with the UN Sustainable Development Goals and is well positioned for inclusion in ESG indices and support 9 out of 17 UN Sustainable Development Goals across 28 ESG Initiatives:

Environmental
- Clean water and sanitation
- Affordable and clean energy
- Responsible consumption and production

Governance
- Reduced inequalities
- Partnerships for the goals

Social
- Quality education
- Gender equality
- Industry, innovation and infrastructure
- Sustainable communities and cities

Environmental Impact: Protecting the Environment

Planet wants to be part of the systemic change in reducing carbon emissions and being a leader in affordable housing towards positive environmental impact. Here is what they are saying and doing to reach these goals:

ENERGY AND CLIMATE CHANGE

Reducing our consumption of energy and increasing the amount of renewable energy that we use will be critical. We already install energy efficient urban infrastructure such as LED street lighting across the entire road length of our projects and a photovoltaic system is installed on the roof of the iconic Innovation Hub building at Smart City Laguna in Brazil. Our houses are being equipped with technology that supports the use of energy monitoring devices, which will allow us to test a monitoring system for residents within the Planet App. We also recently held a course for residents at Laguna which included learning how to read energy-efficiency labels on appliances. Thermal performance evaluations have been carried out on some buildings to help us understand the link between comfort and energy use and to test the possibility of integrating renewable energy, particularly from micro-wind turbines and photovoltaic systems. In the coming years we intend to increase energy monitoring, introduce new site management strategies and more energy measuring devices, and identify more energy-saving building techniques. We also plan to carry out energy performance evaluations on all building types that we develop. In September 2021, we began a partnership with The Polytechnic University of Turin (Italian: Politecnico di Torino) to help us achieve our energy consumption, waste, water and biodiversity goals. It will also help us to align our business units with ESG in order to reach GRESB standards in the next three years.

WASTE MINIMISATION

An area where Planet is making real strides is in reducing the disposal of soil to landfill during construction by prioritising the natural topography and by reusing excavation material for road paving and landscaping. More than a million cubic metres of material will be reused at Laguna, for example. We also use industry-leading BIM software to help us optimise the use of materials. We plan to improve the monitoring of waste management, increase the use of measuring devices, and identify and integrate technologies that will support our waste management and recycling efforts.

WATER EFFICIENCY

The impact of global warming coupled with an ever-growing population means water is among our most precious resources. We must increase our water efficiency and innovate to manage our water resources better. One of the main aspects of the design of our Smart Cities is the creation of stormwater storage as a collection point for the overall drainage system. This is integrated into the landscaping design as a lagoon, becoming a permanent water supply source from the construction phase. At Laguna, for example, where the lagoon has the capacity to store 90,000/100,000m3 of rainwater, it is reused in concrete production and road construction. Another example is the lagoon at Smart City Natal in Brazil, which will have a stormwater storage capacity of 37,000m3 integrated into the green areas. We usually collaborate with local municipalities to improve infrastructure, whether for water, energy, waste or biodiversity. We will continue our focus on water efficiency through greater monitoring of use and the introduction of new technology, and by encouraging water reuse.

LAND USE AND BIODIVERSITY

Biodiversity is essential to the provision of nutritious food, clean water and protection from extreme events. The way we use land can have a significant impact on biodiversity. Therefore, we evaluate earthworks to reduce potential sediment discharge and erosion risk and we introduce green areas into all our designs. Our urban landscape design prioritises native vegetation (which is partially relocated within the development) which can promote the ecosystem. We have also introduced hundreds of thousands of square metres of permeable concrete pavement for walkways, driveways and parking lots to increase stormwater infiltration and reduce potential run-off. We support nature conservation through our guidelines for best practice in urban landscaping. At Laguna and Aquiraz in Brazil, for example, the lagoons have created their own ecosystems and improved the quality of the local environment.

Planet's ESG agenda and goals of making their homes "futureproof" would not be possible without their Digital infrastructure.

Three Categories of Digital Comprise the Offering to the Planet Communities:

i. Subscriptions to the following:
    a. Smart Infrastructure in a box or Smart Home Automation in a box
    b. Maintenance predictive analytics
    c. Community Energy Savings

    d. Automated Resident Engagement

    e. Entrepreneurship programming for women and youth

2. Marketplace:
   a. Maintenance Payment
   b. Grocery and non-food retail order and delivery
   c. Freight Integration and bulk delivery
   d. Discounts with partners
   e. Ride Hailing (carpooling) and other travel
   f. Access to doctors and healthcare

3. Data
   a. Gamification of interaction between residents and marketplace
   b. Financial access to the marketplace

Planet allows residents to enjoy "Smart-Home" management through an App called the Planet Smart City App. Through this App residents can do the following:

- Enter their home without keys … they can enter their home with the Planet App
- Manage and pay utility bills
- Report and schedule maintenance
- Manage security
- Connect with neighbours
- Book amenities such as courses, football pitches, rooms for celebrations such as birthday parties
- Find out what is going on in the community and attend community events and activities
- Rent and access products from the Library of Things
- Access partner discounts in the marketplace such as discounts on haircuts, pizza, home appliances and sporting equipment

All of this is meant to give families the chance to live fulfilling lives and create strong, connected communities. It is a commitment to work towards the highest environmental, social and governance (ESG) standards. Planet has created something new; a solution to give many more families the chance of a decent home while reducing construction and household emissions and other environmental impacts.

AUDREY KLEIN holds various Non-Exec Board roles and is Chair of the ESG Committee for Planet Smart City and SFO Capital Partners. She is also a member of the audit committee for Planet Smart City and a Senior Advisor to McKinsey in Real Estate. She has held various Head of Fundraising positions but is best known for starting the European business out of London for Park Hill Real Estate, a division of Blackstone which she ran for 9 years.

PLANET SMART CITY has created a new category of technologically enabled affordable housing and is generating market leading returns. Planet is the only real estate developer that brings the "smart city concept" to affordable housing neighbourhoods and is the first smart affordable housing product in the world. Planet is seizing the opportunity to capitalise on a highly fragmented market. Planet Smart City is disrupting the Affordable Housing Market and making peoples' lives better.

BRIAN KLINKSIEK
& SIMON MARX

LaSalle

WHAT THE PANDEMIC HAS CHANGED – AND THE 15-MINUTE-CITY MISSES – ABOUT THE FUTURE OF CITIES

With more time spent working from home during the pandemic, the idea of the "15-Minute City" has captured imaginations. The concept pre-dates the pandemic but it has gained traction in the wake of it. Popularised by French academic Carlos Moreno, it idealises the ability to satisfy most wants and needs within a short distance of home. Rather than promoting traditional suburbanisation, the concept holds that many of the activities of life, from working, shopping, dining, exercising, engaging in culture, learning, and going to the doctor should be able to be accomplished within neighbourhoods where no point is more than 15 minutes away by foot or bike.

Could this be a model for the best way to organise successful cities? Or a litmus test for the most attractive places to invest in real estate?

It is true that many cities – particularly those which are geographically constrained, rapidly expanding, or driven by government policy – integrate live, work, and play into mixed-use areas. But in practice, most precincts specialise in one or two of these activities. This may be due to historic, cultural, or simply practical reasons.

The limitations of the 15-minute ideal start to show when considering activities that benefit the most from bringing a large, critical mass of diverse people together. For instance, can you really support high-quality live drama, live music, and professional sport entirely within the confines of a single 15-minute city? Or can every 15-minute city support a truly diverse range of cuisines and experiences, and specialised healthcare and advanced education? Within any one existing or imagined 15-minute city, it's hard to fathom achieving the scale possible to make all types of face-to-face activities work; there are simply not enough people with the same interests or needs.

To support the full range of urban offerings, we need the metropolitan scale typical of a major city region, along with a degree of intraurban travel – in other words, commuting. But in a world where physical and virtual space are in intense competition, the traditional bedroom suburb and the commuter city centre must change. For physical places to capture their fair share of activity despite the cost, in both money and time, of commuting, they must bring something special to the table.

Let's start with areas once called suburbs. To thrive, they will have to become more like 15-minute cities. The term we've been applying at LaSalle to these areas is Liveable Zones. With attractive housing, strong schools and open spaces, these areas have the whole spectrum of amenities needed for daily living. Illustrative examples include urban villages like Wimbledon, as well as satellite cities like Milton Keynes. These will thrive as technology allows more people to spend more time at or close to home. The most successful Liveable Zones are those which help to tackle social inequality by offering a wide range of housing types at various price points across socioeconomically and racially integrated neighbourhoods, with easy and equitable access to quality education.

Parts of these Liveable Zones can be focal points for local activity, such as shopping, entertainment, or education. But because these areas face practical limitations in terms of amenities, infrastructure, and catchment size, another type of place is needed to facilitate the more rarefied forms of in-person interaction and experience. These places, which might traditionally be called city centres or downtowns, but we call Confluence

Zones, are rich in amenities, including bars, restaurants, museums, and other uses that benefit from in-person experience, such as collaborative offices and landmark retail stores. A fear of missing out ('FOMO') on social and cultural attractions draws in significant footfall.

Investors in Confluence Zones must remain creative in attracting the consumers and workers to their properties, especially as economies reopen. While demand for the attractions of Confluence Zones is high, societal preferences around them have changed. For example, staff going back to the office will demand modern workplaces with strong environmental credentials that promote employee welfare. Extra provision needs to be made for engagement and inspiration to offset the challenges associated with commuting and congestion. People in collaborative roles with a need for face-to-face interaction will benefit most from a return to a centralised office, whilst those in more focussed or operational roles will not abandon their home office so readily, concentrating office demand in the most successful Confluence Zones.

There is a third type of zone. Adjacent Zones act as overflow areas for both Confluence and Liveable Zones; their main source of value is proximity to other areas. Without offering the wide spectrum of experiential amenities typically associated with Confluence Zones nor the comforting liveability of Liveable Zones, Adjacent Zones may house uses such as urban logistics, affordable housing, retail parks, and self-storage centres. Investors will also target these zones should they anticipate a gentrification that leads to its transformation into a Liveable or Confluence Zone. But these areas will be most susceptible to market share shifts toward virtual ways of interacting, rendering offices in Adjacent Zones particularly at risk.

In summary, we're proposing a new way to think about how we use cities that moves beyond traditional concepts like suburbs and downtowns. While the 15-minute city is too sub-scale to realise the full benefits of urban agglomeration, an old model of peripheral to central commuting fails to acknowledge the realities of an increasingly hybrid world that blends in-person and virtual interaction. Specifically, we observe that some areas tend to specialise in facilitating in-person collaboration, whereas others focus on home life. For real estate investors and developers, factoring in these considerations will be critical when determining whether assets are economically viable. Understanding the suitability of an asset type and tenant's core activity in relation to the zone they are in, can help identify investment and divestment opportunities, as well as shape asset management strategies.

BRIAN KLINKSIEK is Head of European Research and Global Portfolio Strategies at LaSalle and is a member of all LaSalle investment committees in Europe. Prior to joining LaSalle in 2020, over nearly 17 years Mr Klinksiek held various research and strategy leadership roles at Heitman, with diverse experience across a wide range of markets and property sectors in Europe, North America and Asia. Brian holds a BA with honors and distinction from Stanford University, and an MBA with high honors from the Booth School of Business at the University of Chicago.

SIMON MARX is a managing director in LaSalle's European Research & Strategy team. His primary function is to monitor the European property markets; including defining fund strategies, identifying acquisition opportunities and bringing new sources of global capital to Europe. Prior to joining LaSalle in 2011, Simon was Head of UK Analytics at the listed property information company CoStar. Simon completed a BSc (Hons) in French & German at the University of Salford, followed by an MSc in Real Estate Investment & Finance at the University of Reading.

LASALLE INVESTMENT MANAGEMENT is one of the world's leading real estate investment managers. On a global basis, we manage approximately $77 billion of assets in private equity, debt and public real estate investments as of Q3 2021. The firm sponsors a complete range of investment vehicles including open- and closed-end funds, separate accounts and indirect investments. Our diverse client base includes public and private pension funds, insurance companies, governments, corporations, endowments and private individuals from across the globe. For more information please visit www.lasalle.com and LinkedIn.

MELANIE LEECH

British Property Federation

The town centre of the future will be at once familiar and radically different in ways we may not yet imagine.

Familiar because ultimately town centres are shaped by us. High streets are the lifeblood of communities and have always had to be flexible and adapt to changing consumer preferences and habits.

Many of our high streets and town centres are currently retail-led and this will need to change as the retail footprint continues to shrink and retail continues to evolve. One key shift we will see is a move from traditional retail to experiential retail as businesses look to leverage experience over products – something that cannot be replicated online.

There'll be a wider mix of activities along the high streets of the future – homes, community venues and amenities alongside an office infrastructure whose evolution into higher quality, more flexible spaces has been accelerated by Covid-19.

Overall however this process of constant re-invention and development is a long-term organic evolution, not a revolution or knee jerk response to short term pressures such as the Covid-19 pandemic or to the kind of quick fixes politicians often look for.

Piecemeal changes to planning through permitted development rights have spurred on change of uses in our high streets but replacing a shop for a café or even an office, serves no purpose if people are not drawn into the area or well-served by it. Local authorities need to step back and articulate and re-assert a sense of place – defined and owned locally.

Where there are poor quality buildings – changing their use will merely perpetuate that lack of quality and short-change everyone in the local community. And bringing buildings up to standard and retrofitting them to deliver on net zero targets will involve close collaboration between tenants and landlords – underpinned and supported by policy incentives and levers such as the zero-rating of VAT on repairs and maintenance that the BPF has consistently called for.

It's not just the bricks and mortar in town centres that need careful planning, the transport and digital infrastructure to support businesses, and now more than ever homes, is essential to creating viable places with thriving local economies.

We also need policy that recognises the vital role that urban warehousing plays in meeting online shopping demands. The allocation of land for housing has restricted development of industrial space – just as a surge in ecommerce is pushing demand to record levels. The solution is a more creative approach to land intensification – such as multi-level or mixed-use warehousing – and policy that supports this.

Perhaps most importantly of all is the need for social infrastructure. Town and city centres are hubs of social interaction – safe, inclusive spaces that will increasingly be pedestrianised with green spaces and buildings promoting health and wellbeing.

So – on the one hand familiarity in the sense that the facilities and environment we know today will evolve and respond to how we decide we want to live our lives. But on the other hand – just as with other parts of our life – innovation and technology have the potential to re-shape our town and city centres in ways we can't yet understand.

Without heading to the realms of science fiction – think about the way in which mobile communications have developed over the last few years. The concept of connected cities is still arguably in its infancy (at least here in the UK) and try to extrapolate where the same kind of technological development might take us in – say – 25 years' time. Personally I find it hard to imagine what the limits of this might be and how that might shape the way we live and the places that underpin our lives.

My two sons take for granted that technology will continually develop and provide better, faster and more intuitive products to support their lives. Creating and evolving the built environment has always been seen – and is – a process led by long-term thinking and investment decisions. So one of the challenges for the property sector of today – and tomorrow – will be how to create lasting assets that also continuously evolve.

––––––––––––

MELANIE LEECH has been the Chief Executive of the British Property Federation since 2015. Her role is to champion a diverse, successful and sustainable real estate UK real estate sector recognised for the positive benefits it delivers to communities across the country. Melanie began her working life as a Police Constable in the Metropolitan Police Service and held a number of senior roles in the civil service before spending 10 years as Director General of the Food and Drink Federation. Melanie is also a Trustee of the property industry charity LandAid and a member of the Council of the University of Essex. She was awarded a CBE in 2015 for services to the food and drink industry.

The BRITISH PROPERTY FEDERATION (BPF) represents the real estate sector, an industry which contributes more than £100bn to the economy in 2019 and directly employs more than 1 million people. The BPF's membership comprises a broad range of owners, managers and developers of real estate as well as those who support them. Their investments help drive the UK's economic success, provide essential infrastructure and create great places where people can live, work and relax.

KIRK LINDSTROM

Round Hill Capital

PUTTING REAL PEOPLE AT THE HEART OF THE TOWN OF THE FUTURE

The Town of the Future will be shaped by you, the next generation of real estate investors and developers, and I am optimistic that you will prioritise the need to create homes that strengthen communities, not weaken them, and that balance individuals' needs with global environmental and social challenges.

Across Europe, our cities, but more particularly our towns have been shaped and defined by histories that go back hundreds or even thousands of years. Even where housing stock has been redeveloped we are fitting urban footprints reflecting lifestyles that pre-date automobiles and the electric light.

Traditionally a town was a sizeable settlement centred around a market square, where goods and services could be traded. In recent centuries, that definition has been challenged as many towns have been subsumed within the urban sprawl of our cities, from Hammersmith in London to Gateshead in Newcastle. Often what has been lost is more than an arbitrary boundary, it has been a sense of community.

Towns, whether standing separate or as districts within a larger urban area, fulfil an essential role in human behaviour, providing local access at a human scale to meet our fundamental needs for company and community, fresh air and outside spaces. These were factors that post-war town planners of the 1960s and 70s were aware of, and sought to service through blocks of flats that replaced traditional low density housing with space for open urban areas and ring roads. Sadly many of these experiments failed, suffering from high crime rates and seeing distinctive market squares and highstreets replaced with chain stores and out of town business parks accessible only by car.

As we move into the second quarter of this century, our industry needs fresh ideas and fresh thinkers to help reshape our dwellings and towns to match modern lifestyles with a sense of belonging, purpose and fun. Technology has reshaped how we work, live and play and imposed both new challenges and opportunities for living space. Outside of city centres, local high streets have faltered, light industry and brutalist apartments have fallen into disrepair while suburban sprawl sees many struggle from a lack of infrastructure. As a result more than 25,000 hectares of brownfield land lies fallow within the UK's towns and cities.

In the years ahead, many of you will be at the forefront of reshaping tomorrow's towns. The traditional student move out of halls into private accommodation in the second and third years of university has in recent years shifted away from poorly converted shared homes, to shared apartments with modern facilities and lively communities. In cities such as Newcastle, neighbourhoods famous for their student populations such as Jesmond are benefiting from sensitive conversions and developments, and I am excited about how your living experiences will play through into your future attitudes to co-living developments as you enter the working world.

Co-living is not a new concept, but a focus on affordable, quality, privately developed and operated co-living is. Cities traditionally renowned for the vibrancy of their urban populations such as New York and Berlin have attempted to impose rent controls to sustain the character of their populations, and the wide array of services and entertainment they rely upon. By artificially capping prices, incentives to invest and improve were impacted, but now the tide is turning and an exciting urban renaissance is occurring in cities such as San Francisco, London, Paris and Berlin. As local authorities, investors and developers work together to reshape tomorrow's towns and cities, I believe that more and more local residents will be keen to view their homes as hubs for their community lives rather than castles in which to isolate themselves and their families.

Denser urban populations in modern, energy efficient homes with strong public transport links have environmental as well as sociological benefits. Cohabiting families are one of the fastest growing housing types in the UK, and modern housing developments often feature shared amenities providing for more affordable private spaces and the pursuit of hobbies. Whether for students, families or senior living, where we live shapes us and the quality of our lives.

I believe that the next generation of real estate professionals will continue to put real human needs at the heart of their decision making. By truly understanding how people live in their dwellings our next industry leaders will improve not only quality of life, but also our impact on the planet. As tomorrow's real estate professionals you have a big responsibility, and I am confident you will be up to the challenge.

KIRK LINDSTROM is Round Hill's Chief Investment Officer and he has over 20 years of experience in real estate, banking and corporate finance. Kirk has previously held senior positions at some of the world's top investment firms. Prior to joining Round Hill, he was a Managing Director in Goldman Sachs' European real estate investment banking team. His experience includes advising clients on transactions totalling over €20bn in the real estate and lodging industries.

⊣H⊢ ROUND HILL CAPITAL

Founded in 2002 by CEO Michael Bickford, ROUND HILL CAPITAL (RHC) is a leading global specialist real estate investor, developer and manager, with a global asset portfolio spanning across the US and Europe. Since inception it has acquired and repositioned for long-term institutional ownership over 135,000 residential units and student housing beds. RHC is a responsible landlord of assets offering housing to a range of occupants, from students through to senior citizens. It also has an established track record of positive returns and invests in, and manages real estate on behalf of some of the world's leading institutions and private investors.

EMMA MACKENZIE

NewRiver REIT

The Town of the Future will do what town centres across the UK have always done – provide a sense of place, belonging and community.

The global pandemic has pronounced the role of the town centre and community. It has enhanced local social responsibility and the appreciation that for a town to thrive, it must be used and enjoyed. People need their local town centre to meet their day-to-day needs. They want it to be inviting, clean, accessible, safe and well-maintained; but these should be the accepted basics. They also want it to be unique and surprising yet familiar, and a place they can be proud to call home.

With advances in technology increasingly affecting how we interact with the world, there is no doubt that the future town centre will have exciting new digital innovations, some of which perhaps have not even been invented yet.

However, a town centre will never be run by robots, for robots. A town centre will always be a community hub for human beings to go about their daily lives, a place where people of all ages live, shop, work, socialise, relax and engage with cultural activities. Open green spaces will be key.

A BRIEF HISTORY

The real estate sector is a critical driving force behind how town centres evolve. The sector responds to changing social needs, including the move from cellular offices to open plan; accommodating the growth of national retailers in the 1980s with the development of shopping centres; giant food stores and retailers expanding in out-of-town locations; and more recently, demand for large distribution warehouses on motorway networks to fulfil online purchases.

Most occupiers of commercial space do not own their buildings, they rent them from private or publicly listed landlords who own the property as an investment to derive income. The occupiers lease their space rather than buy it to avoid capital being tied up in property. The real estate industry wants town centres to be incubators for businesses to thrive. Property owners are willing to invest in the aesthetics of town centre buildings to ensure a relevant and sustainable future.

PHYSICAL STORES AND ONLINE

Pre-pandemic town centres were experiencing increasing vacancy thanks to various factors but most notably the rise of online retail which now accounts for approximately 30% of all retail sales. Covid has of course accelerated this change. Retailers no longer need representation in as many locations and the role of department stores is no longer relevant. What will become of this vacant space?

As always, the real estate sector will respond to the changing demands from consumers and occupiers, repurposing space to accommodate new and exciting uses. Homes will emerge with people living in the heart of town centres again. There will be inspiring and flexible offices that accommodate the new office/home hybrid working. There will be leisure facilities with restaurants, cafes and bars to help drive an evening economy; convenient medical services and there will always be retail at the heart of a town centre giving people the opportunity to see and touch goods before they buy and most importantly, fulfil the very basic human need to interact with other people.

PROPERTY JOBS HELP SHAPE THE FUTURE

There are many careers within the real estate sector that will play important roles in helping shape the town centre of the future. From architects, planners, building and quantity surveyors, engineers, asset managers, (think Lego and Monopoly combined!) environmental specialists to accountants, marketeers, data analysts, builders and lawyers. Regardless of skillset and ability there's a career for all in the property sector. It is a dynamic industry with people and teamwork at its heart, helping shape the places we live, work and play in.

NewRiver are a listed property company specialising in owning, managing, and developing essential and resilient retail assets. Our retail destinations provide everyday goods and services to local communities, i.e. things a household needs including food, toiletries, banks, opticians, cafes, hairdressers and pharmacies. Increasingly we are providing alternative uses in our assets including gyms, libraries, doctors' surgeries, flexi offices and hotels. We are invested in over 50 communities across the UK and our 50-strong team work hard, supported by specialist advisors and local Councils, to innovate our assets to ensure they provide essential goods and services for the local community whilst creating a place people can get together and enjoy.

Town centres are a barometer of society and are always adapting to the way we live. The real estate industry has the privilege to be part of shaping our towns of the future and we must work together to make it happen. It's a very exciting and defining time to be a part of the property industry!

As Head of Asset Management and ESG, **EMMA MACKENZIE** has overarching responsibility for NewRiver's financial and operational portfolio performance, property management and the Company's Environmental, Social and Governance programme. Emma is a qualified chartered surveyor with over 20 years' experience in retail property. Emma is a Board member of the High Street Task Force which provides guidance to help communities and local governments transform their high streets and Emma also sits on the Commercial Committee of the British Property Federation.

**NEW
RIVER**

NEWRIVER REIT is a leading Real Estate Investment Trust specialising in owning, managing and developing resilient retail assets across the UK that provide essential goods and services whilst supporting the development of thriving communities. For more information about NewRiver REIT plc visit www.nrr.co.uk

CALLUM MCDOUGALL

Mason Owen

The Town of the Future will ... depend less on retail.

The high street within most Town centres was historically the main and only destination to shop, eat, and socialise. However, over the last few decades, many traditional high streets have been in a steady decline due to a revolution in the way we now shop as a society. This decline has been accelerated by the recent impacts of the Coronavirus pandemic.

Due to significant strides made in technology, it is only too easy for us to use a laptop, phone or tablet to order goods and have these delivered straight to our doorstep without the need to travel. This could include clothes, electronics, food etc. The same can be said for how society manages their banking. The expansion and convenience of online banking has led to a vast number of branches being obsolete and no longer required.

Given such technological advances and the emergence of convenience retailing (e.g. out of town shopping centres, retail parks), Towns of the future will need to adapt quickly to this societal change. Both private and public sector stakeholders will need to explore ways in which they are able to utilise redundant retail space to re-imagine and re-purpose this for the community's benefit.

OFFER GREATER CONVENIENCE

Most UK Town centres traditionally comprise a long single high street with Council owned parking nearby, which most communities must pay to use. With the insurgence of out of town shopping centres and retail parks, it is vital that where feasible, both public and private sector stakeholders work together to improve access into Town centres for their local community but also re-generate sections of their Town centres where needed to improve convenience.

DEPEND MORE ON LEISURE AND FOOD OFFERINGS

Communities want to shop and socialise locally if they can. However, it is vital that Towns of the Future offer an experience and value that negates the community from travelling for the same service.

The decline in the retail sector and subsequent deflation of market rents within this sector over the last few years has opened up the way for great local independents to emerge and provide a unique offering to their communities, which they could not get if they travelled elsewhere. I lose count of how many fantastic places to eat, drink and socialise there are in my Town and all are run by local people. It is important that Towns of the future continue to support local and independent businesses because they will ultimately become the beating heart of their communities and draw people into Town centres.

It is important that, where feasible, Towns of the future establish more green areas to promote leisure activities. Existing leisure facilities should be maintained and if feasible, expanded or re-generated to become more accessible for their local community.

OFFER GREATER VOLUMES OF RESIDENTIAL HOUSING

The restrictions in planning and permitted development have been softened over the years, which has created greater opportunities for residential development for both the private and public sectors. Whether this be housing or more likely within Towns, Apartment complexes. A number of local authorities are under pressure to hit government set housing targets, but are struggling to find possible sites to develop within their communities.

Where feasible, The Town of the Future will utilise all existing or redundant brownfield sites to create more housing. Where retail space has become obsolete, stakeholders should be looking at converting poorly utilised spaces to residential if feasible to do so. A great example of re-generation in reality is the Wirral Waters re-generation masterplan: www.wirralwaters.co.uk/masterplan.

BE MORE ENERGY EFFICIENT

Climate change is a significant problem for our planet. The way in which society now constructs and makes use of buildings is undergoing a slow but progressive renascence to allow for greater efficiency in terms of carbon output and waste. This is forced in part by the ever constricting legalisation being set by national Government (e.g. Energy Act 2011, The Energy Efficiency (Private Rented Property) (England and Wales) Regulations 2015).

Towns of the future will need to promote sustainable methods of construction in line with Government legislation, with existing buildings improving energy efficiency where possible.

CALLUM MCDOUGALL: I am a Chartered Surveyor working within the Asset Management team at Mason Owen. I currently manage an expansive nationwide commercial property portfolio for various clients, undertaking a variety of professional work including site inspection, rent collection, maintenance management, lease management and service charge consultancy/ delivery. Moreover, I provide professional advice to both landlords and tenants on matters of lease renewals, rent reviews, leasing and letting of commercial premises.

mason owen...
property consultants

MASON OWEN is a firm of Chartered Surveyors based in Liverpool, specialising in commercial property services to include:

- Retail & Leisure Agency
- Business Premises & Industrial Agency
- Investment
- Asset Management
- Landlord & Tenant

Some of Mason Owen's biggest clients include Vabeld UK Ltd, LXI REIT, Iceland Foods, Greggs, Screwfix and the Co-operative.

DOMINIC MOORE

Clearbell

The Town of the Future will be… green and community focussed. Embracing the huge leaps in technology will drive our urban areas to be people focussed. For too long the focus has been on getting road traffic in, out and around town centres rather than how to enable actual people to get around. Only recently are we seeing a true shift away from car based movements to other means of mobility. This is where the biggest change in our towns will be seen. A glimpse over to Holland can show how it can be done and to quote an official from Utrecht "Our revenue is healthy people, less traffic and beautiful living". Sounds good. However this will only take place with willing local authorities able to fund required infrastructure and public transport. In the push to reduce our carbon emissions the dominance of car based travel has to be tackled head-on.

The shared space that any urban environment has is pretty limited and should therefore make sure it accommodates people first. Take a look around your local town and see how much space is dedicated to cars. Then think how better that space could be used if the number of cars was significantly reduced. Suddenly there is ample room for trams, bus lanes, cycle lanes, gardens, parks, public buildings and housing. A town providing space for all of its community is a town that thrives as people want to be there. With people comes prosperity. A town centre that is attractive and full of people will drive commerce and hence jobs.

Another shift that is happening right now is the ability for people to work from home more. The significance this has on local businesses, particularly retailers, is worth noting. One of the positives to come out of the pandemic period is that local shops have thrived. All of that local spend has not disappeared off to the big city centres. With people now having a blend of working from home and commuting to the office we will see a balancing of spending between local shops and city centre outlets. This is a positive for your local high street and has seen a growth in small local businesses that will hopefully continue.

Retail is changing rapidly with the rise of online shopping and home delivery. The result is that towns might not need the same number of shop outlets that they once did. This could benefit the housing stock if these premises are converted. However we are seeing a demand for more experiential retailing. Things like indoor golf or cricket, small cinemas, gyms, yoga studios and indoor kids play areas, plus the usual food and drink, can make use of those old shops and provide a local community with required services. So the make up of your local high street will change. Goods that can be easily bought online and delivered will be less prevalent and there will be more focus on activities that you can't do online.

The further greening of our towns will come in how we procure our energy. Renewable technology is advancing quickly and having small scale renewable energy sources at home will become common place. I expect planning laws to ensure that all new buildings have an element of renewable energy within their design. Perhaps now is the time to see public spaces and buildings used more effectively to provide a local source of energy. This could potentially be pooled to provide a municipal source that the local authority can manage and create an income stream from.

Allied to reducing our carbon emissions is the re-use of existing building stock. For too long older buildings have been demolished to make way for larger developments that don't always add to the local street scene. Given the emphasis on embodied carbon within existing structures, and not releasing that back into the atmosphere through the activities involved in demolition and rebuilding, we are at a time where older buildings will be sympathetically re-imagined and re-used. This can create a link to the past for local communities and perhaps create a better sense of "Place" for any town. Our heritage is important in creating a community.

And finally the most precious commodity in any urban environment are the spaces that aren't built on. Parks, squares, woods, commons and recs are vitally important to any community. These will continue to be treasured and ensuring that they are integral to the town's urban landscape is essential. Even in the most built up locations the area loved the most is the part not built on. Green shines through.

———————————

DOMINIC MOORE joined Clearbell in 2009 and is responsible for the asset management of all investments and for integrating our Sustainability Policy into everything we do. Dom began his 25+ year career with a postgraduate diploma in Property Valuation and Management from Sheffield Hallam University and a BSc (Hons) in Geology from The University of Liverpool. Outside work, Dom enjoys running, cycling and spending time with his wife and two children.

Clearbell

CLEARBELL is a leading UK specialist real estate fund management and advisory business. We have invested in, developed, and managed over £2.3bn of assets across a diverse range of sectors for both Funds and Separate Mandates.

ED
PROTHEROE

AREF

Some leading lights in the real estate investment industry helped me write this; people that will be influencing how The Town of the Future will be moulded. The core theme was around the environment. Not only the climate crisis but our social environment and the impact the buildings these folks invest in have on that.

First, I asked Miranda, a colleague's 11¾-year-old daughter, for her view. Interestingly, she believes that while towns and cities evolve over the years, it's important that they should preserve their history. She wants towns to be beautiful, yet practical. How do her ideas compare to those of my panel of experts?

The single greatest issue towns of the future will face is undoubtedly climate change – described by one expert as 'humanity's greatest challenge'. The real estate industry has a major role to play in saving our environment.

First, consider this:

1. Our government, along with many others around the world, has pledged to substantially reduce greenhouse gas (GHG) emissions and achieve net zero carbon by 2050;
2. Over 40% of GHG emissions come from the built environment – the buildings we all use to live, learn, work, shop and play in;
3. Around 80% of the total building stock in 2050 has already been built.

GHG emissions come from heating, air-conditioning, lighting and electrical devices we use in our homes, offices, schools, shops etc. But also from how they were built – in making all that steel, glass, bricks and concrete.

So, the real estate industry must think very carefully about how they construct buildings in future, using more sustainable materials. While at the same time, we need to substantially reduce emissions from the existing building stock.

We could see complete electrification and a greater use of sustainable natural resources. For example, it is possible to use local rivers as cooling systems and more space used for renewable energy. Think of all that roof space in your town and how many solar panels could be fitted to generate clean electricity.

Much greater provision for electric vehicle (EV) charging is already underway. We are starting to see charging points in public car parks, supermarkets, retail parks and office parks.

This renewed focus on sustainable investing isn't just coming from the industry's desire to do the right thing. More and more environmental regulation is expected to come through too. So the industry is acting now, to future-proof their investments.

As part of this focus on the environment, the investment industry is also looking at the broader social impact their properties may have for the future. There seems to be a shift in mindset, as they try to really understand how a town needs to operate in order to thrive. The COVID pandemic has focussed minds on how buildings affect occupants. This is a noticeable move away from predominantly financial considerations in the investment industry.

There is a clear focus on the need to better utilise the current buildings and space available. So this is less about new buildings – think carbon – and more about repurposing current stock. Expect to see more mixed-use space, both in terms of areas in town and specific buildings.

There will be a move away from distinct areas for retail, offices or residential, with these merging in the future. Buildings themselves are likely to become more mixed use. Office buildings are being converted to include residential and retail space, for example. Another concept being considered is the 15 minute city, where most of the things you need on any day are within just a 15 minute walk. A return to the 'local way of life'?

This might be an appropriate moment to briefly reflect on history. Towns evolved through the 19th century, with a view to people's wellbeing, planned with parks, libraries, communal baths etc. Through the 20th century this included medical centres and post offices for example. Since the '90s, however, planning and developing has lacked such 'master plan', with little or no specific space for people's needs. The real estate industry, town planners and government need to collaborate to rediscover this level of thinking. Perhaps Miranda had it right.

I sense a genuine change in the status quo, a realisation that more recent past practices are unsustainable – in every sense. The industry is finding new ways forward that sound highly beneficial for people in the towns of the future.

The next generation of real estate professional is going to be key in this process. The future of our towns will be directly in their hands. As one member of the panel put it, she has the opportunity to turn what she cares about into a career.

So, dear reader, how do you see The Town of the Future? What have we missed? Maybe The Town of the Future will… need you!

ED PROTHEROE started his City career in 1984, aged 18, so now has nearly 40 years of experience in the fund management industry. He consults for and acts on behalf of AREF on several Board initiatives around communications, strategy and business development. Before founding consulting firm Parkview Capital Ltd in Feb 2017, he had senior franchise and business management roles at M&G Investments and M&G Real Estate. He has also been Head of Research at a boutique broker and, previously, was an award-winning pan-European equities fund manager at Aberdeen Asset Management.

The **ASSOCIATION OF REAL ESTATE FUNDS** (AREF) represents the UK real estate funds industry and has around 60 member funds with a collective net asset value of more than £64 billion under management on behalf of their investors. The Association is committed to promoting transparency in performance measurement and fund reporting through the AREF Code of Practice, the MSCI/AREF UK Quarterly Property Funds Index and the AREF Property Fund Vision Handbook. You can view more information by visiting our website: www.aref.org.uk.

CHRIS RADLEY

Fletcher Priest

The Town of the Future will… hopefully be largely with us already, as an adaptation of existing urban spaces responding to changes in our climate, society and economy.

When is the future? At Fletcher Priest, our work always involves speculating and looking towards changing contexts.

The last couple of years have seen big changes in the way people work, shop and socialise (where, how and when), with consequences for society and the economy. This has been partly a result of lockdowns, restrictions and other Covid-19 measures, and partly longer, slower changes bubbling to the surface. Alongside this, humanity's impact on the climate has become increasingly apparent. So in the UK, The Town of the Future will be hotter in the summer, wetter in the winter, and less reliant on predictable flows of workers and shoppers.

It has become easier for many jobs to be done remotely, at least some of the time, and more acceptable for working times to be flexible. I believe the only constant is change and there will be no 'back to normal' reset. This can only be a good thing, giving people more control over how and where they spend their time, however it is having real consequences for the way our urban environments are used. Humans are fundamentally social animals – the reason for the success and longevity of cities. Businesses, uses, and spaces have historically been clustered and aggregated. In The Town of the Future these will be more dispersed – both within and between urban areas.

This may sound downbeat, and challenging times are certainly ahead, however as designers we are trained to be optimists and see the opportunities in less than promising situations. For example, the upside of these changes could be greater access to uses for all people, increasing the liveliness and viability of less central areas.

Mitigating climate change can go hand in hand with creating a vibrant, exciting and healthy place to live and work. Buildings can provide habitats for wildlife and plants on their roofs and facades, whilst giving measurable improvements to our wellbeing. Water can be conserved and local temperatures reduced by urban micro-wetlands, risk of flooding reduced by using blue roofs and permeable surfaces to collect and disperse rainwater safely.

The decline of motor vehicles will continue – The Town of the Future will prioritise active and electric travel, supported by a change to more localised workplaces, shops and cultural destinations.

These do not need to be purely functional or technical solutions, but can add joy, excitement and interest into the urban environment. Think of the care and attention that Victorian designers often displayed in their bridges, pumping stations and other pieces of infrastructure.

Towns, buildings and spaces that are designed to be flexible and adaptable, long-lasting and upgradeable are better able to respond to change. This applies to existing buildings, which wherever possible should be adapted to meet our future needs, and new buildings which must think beyond a traditional 50-60 year lifespan to create the desirable historic quarters and civic centres of the future.

Many buildings are currently demolished because their geometry does not suit a different use, their materials are failing and cannot be replaced effectively, or potential compromises in cost or function are rejected. I believe The Town of the Future should embody a different attitude, where we work with the quirks of existing structures to create places with interest and history, thinking beyond the red line of ownership boundaries in a more conscious and directed attempt to create supportive networks of buildings.

Shops could become laboratories, offices could become workshops, cinemas could become education spaces, unused basements could become art galleries, empty rooftops could become urban farms.

This will create localised areas that are much more intensively mixed use, rather than centralised zones with ancillary suburbs. It will be complicated, messy and exciting.

Continuing changes in patterns of work will allow more people to spend more time in their local area, rather than commuting into another town or city. This can help create and support local businesses and hopefully foster a greater sense of community.

During the beginning of the Covid-19 pandemic, Fletcher Priest began Futurework – a piece of research speculating on some of these ideas, and drawing on our experience as architects, urban designers and interior designers. This was developed and discussed with the people we work with, coalescing into a short animation of our vision for The Town of the Future. Search our website to take a look.

We do not think there is one single answer to how the city of the future will look or function. The great thing about working in the real estate industry is we can direct tangible improvements to our environment and, although individually our contributions are relatively small, together our work can add up to much more than just a sum of its parts.

CHRIS RADLEY is an architect with 10 years experience at Fletcher Priest, working on a variety of commercial projects at all design and construction stages. These encompass office, retail and hotel and residential uses at diverse scales, both new-build and refurbishment.

fletcher priest architects
london + kōln + rıga

For over forty years, FLETCHER PRIEST has grown to be one of the largest architecture and design practices in the United Kingdom. We are a 120-strong practice formed of a highly collaborative group of people and led by a partnership with wide ranging internal and external interests. We work across four highly integrated scales of practice: urban design, architecture, interior design and design research. We are known for the quality of our thinking and open-minded approach, delivering considered design strategies and innovative, sustainable solutions, at all project scales.

SHANIL
SHAH

SEGRO

T he Town of the Future will… be shaped by the youth of today, a generation whose upbringing has been intertwined with the fastest technological advancement in human history: they learned to walk whilst the internet was a rare luxury and yet now as they begin to impact society, it is a basic necessity.

The pandemic has not reshaped the future of our towns so much as it has accelerated the evolution into a hybrid model of society that wants digital as well as physical experiences, working and collaborating productively whether at home or in an office. Many traditional services will transition into more convenient virtual offerings and the physical space they leave behind will find new uses.

'Smart' towns and cities will be born, fulfilling a requirement for a human 'experience' centred around green spaces, entertainment and convenience which will fundamentally shift the work-life balance back towards "life". At the heart of this revolution will be the idea of mass participation and collaboration to build an ecosystem that is inclusive and liveable for all, supported by sustainable infrastructure and enabled by instant connectivity. Over the coming years, our role as leaders in property will be to ensure that real estate can adapt to support and enable this next stage of societal development.

The era of social media has meant that the youth of today are now more aware of the issues we face, powerful movements are driving demand for improvements in sustainability and equal opportunities for all. Born from this is the theme of liveability and convenience – the concept of smart 15-minute cities where work, shopping, recreation and residence are within a 15-minute distance is beginning to be at the forefront of planning.

This level of convenience can only be successful through disruptive thinking, innovation and investment into sustainable infrastructure and technology. Buildings will become the enablers of this growth, a bridge between physical and digital. Despite the rise of e-commerce, most sales are still conducted in person, in physical shops. The high street still has an important social function, but it needs to adapt. We are looking at how we can create distribution premises within urban areas which allow low carbon, efficient last mile delivery of goods ordered online, making them part of the high street rather than a competitor to it.

The design of new buildings will be expected to combine sustainable and ethical materials with dynamic technology that leverages live data to optimise the use of resources. They will reduce or eliminate waste to generate positive impacts on our climate and biodiversity. Our skylines will transform from silver to green and vertical gardens will become the norm with structures powered using renewable energy.

For inclusiveness to be achieved, core services such as transport, healthcare and education will also evolve. 15-minute cities will enable shorter commutes with walking and cycling spaces becoming more prominent. Public transportation will become more autonomous and efficient. Electrification of vehicles and smart connected networks of roads will mean personal transportation will become more sustainable, whilst business will have better end-to-end visibility of goods in transit. Healthcare and education will also become a hybrid between virtual and physical offerings.

Humans are social beings; the sense of community remains a vital component of human happiness. The towns of the future will play a crucial role in that, just as they do today, but they need to adapt as societies and their priorities evolve. Our job as creators and owners of real estate is to make sure that the buildings are sustainable, not just in terms of their environmental credentials, but also in terms of being able to serve many purposes and cope with society's changing expectations for where and how people live, work and play.

SHANIL SHAH is an Economics graduate from the University of Birmingham. Joined the KPMG graduate scheme and qualified as a chartered accountant with the ICAEW before moving into commercial finance within the real estate industry, firstly at St Modwen and now at SEGRO.

SEGRO

SEGRO is a UK Real Estate Investment Trust (REIT), listed on the London Stock Exchange and Euronext Paris, and is a leading owner, manager and developer of modern warehouses and industrial property in and around major cities and at key transportation hubs in the UK and in seven other European countries.

MATT
SOFFAIR

LGIM Real Assets

THE TOWN OF THE FUTURE WILL...

The next two decades should herald a fundamental shift in their purpose and infrastructure underpinning our towns. We are in the midst of a **climate emergency** that requires material changes to how we travel, what we buy and the infrastructure required to power our lives. Meanwhile, the **structural change to our high streets** resulting from the growth of e-commerce remains in its infancy, with many town centres still grappling with how to reallocate redundant retail space to other more relevant and under-supplied uses. Finally, over time there has been a growing **dislocation between the function of town centres and the needs of the local community**. The combination of these three challenges necessitates a rethink of the role and structure of our towns.

A LOW CARBON FUTURE

In May 2019, the UK Government enshrined in law the need to bring all greenhouse emissions to net zero by 2050. The implications of this commitment are profound. It requires a rebalancing of the UK's energy mix, decarbonisation of existing infrastructure and buildings along with behavioural change at an individual level. The physical fabric of our towns will need to evolve to meet these commitments, so we should see more (literally!) greener buildings, renewable energy sources and a shift to cleaner modes of transport. The revolution in transport should be particularly visible and tangible; out with the internal combustion engine and our overreliance on personal car travel, in with the electric powered vehicles, and a greater emphasis on public transport, cycling and walking. Towns should enable individuals to access the majority of their daily activities within a (low carbon) travel distance of 15 minutes. Meanwhile, individual behavioural shifts will be necessary to support the transition. 'Nudging' individuals to increasingly focus on repair, reuse and recycle is one such example; the ReTuna shopping mall in Sweden is a great example, representing the first shopping centre solely dedicated to selling recycled, reused, and repaired goods.

The risk of this transition exacerbating social inequalities must be front of mind and mitigated. The shift to a Net Zero Carbon economy will require new industries to emerge and replace polluting industries that are no longer viable in their current form. New skills, training and lifelong learning should be a priority to ensure the transition to The Town of the Future does not leave communities behind.

REPOSITIONING THE FUNCTION OF TOWN CENTRE

The narrative around the death of the high street is well understood and requires limited further explanation. Retail is not dead – there will always be a need for shops that offer convenience, experience or the best value for money – however, the UK has too many shops and a fair estimate would be that as many as a third of all shops need to be repurposed to alternative uses. Town centres have been underpinned by shops for decades, with many other uses pushed to the fringes in recent decades.

What should replace retail? Although, correctly, there is no one size fits all, there is a growing body of work that can provide inspiration. In Stockton-on-Tees, a town which has two shopping centres, the council is combining all tenants into one scheme, with the other being demolished and being converted into a public park. In Poole, part of a department store is being replaced by one of the NHS's first Community Diagnostic Centres, providing a one-stop-shop for health checks, scans and tests to help clear the NHS backlog. Meanwhile, an empty department store in Sheffield has been converted into Kommune, which combines an all-day family-friendly food hall with co-working and a library, art gallery and event space. Creative, locally-orientated solutions to the UK's over-supply of retail space are emerging, but are needed in every town.

LOCAL TOWNS FOR LOCAL PEOPLE

A feature of recent times has been a growing acknowledgement of the need for a more decentralised approach to economic development and policy. Every town has a different history, a different economy and different needs. When debating what the function of the town should be going forwards, solutions must reflect the needs of the local population, whether that be housing, education, healthcare or public space. As a minimum, town centres should incorporate good quality housing, a range of employment opportunities, a focus on health and wellbeing and space for local businesses to thrive. Businesses should think closely how they can intentionally contribute directly to the development and wellbeing of the place in which they operate. And, crucially, local people should have the opportunity to grow, work, make and play in the town in which they live and have the capacity to take some ownership in curating what the future of their town should look like.

The Town of the Future should be greener, more local and packed full of different uses. Whether it will be depends on all kinds of people from different backgrounds, different ages and with different skills and interests working together. Will you be part of it?

———————————

MATT SOFFAIR is responsible for leading LGIM Real Assets' research into the retail, leisure and hotel sectors. Matt's role involves advising on portfolio's investment strategies, providing market analysis and forward-looking views, and overseeing the consumer insight and analytics function within the retail and leisure sector. Prior to LGIM, Matt worked directly with a range of retail, leisure and FMCG operators on their location and customer acquisition strategies.

LEGAL & GENERAL INVESTMENT MANAGEMENT REAL ASSETS (LGIMRA) is a division of Legal & General Investment Management (LGIM), one of Europe's largest institutional asset managers and a major global investor. LGIMRA has assets under management of £35.6 billion* and is one of the largest private markets investment managers in the UK. LGIMRA actively invests in and manages assets across commercial, operational and residential property sectors, as well as infrastructure, real estate, corporate and alternative debt.

DIRK SOSEF

Prologis

Urbanisation will shape future city landscapes, bringing with it a greater need for smart infrastructure and solid logistics planning. Bigger and busier cities must focus on logistics innovation in the best locations, to keep goods flowing more efficiently and sustainably.

Everything material you see around you today has been stored in a warehouse. As population centres become ever more concentrated, modern life is made possible thanks to a complex and evolving logistics ecosystem that keeps goods flowing and people looked after. In the UK alone, over 30.000 people work under the roofs of Prologis warehouses, supporting households in growing urban areas, which is only set to increase as towns expand.

From a supply chain perspective, rising migration towards cities inevitably necessitates better infrastructure provision. It's estimated that by 2030, 60% of the world population will live in urban areas and more than 30% of cities will have over a million inhabitants, higher in UK at 83%[1]. Driven by economic prospects, migration to urban areas is unlikely to slow. London for instance, forecast as the fourth largest global economic hotspot attracts a steady inflow of investment, business and residents, meaning more movements of goods and people for the existing infrastructure.

The more people in one place, the greater the need for efficient services and product delivery. Factor in changing online consumption habits, transport needs and a swing towards greater ecommerce reliance, towns of the future will need to evolve to overcome subsequent congestion to accommodate more people commuting, goods moving and logistics. As an example, London is already the most congested city in the world, with drivers on average stuck in jams for 146 hours in 2021[2].

Growing urbanisation will intensify how we designate living, work, and leisure space, making balancing these different functions one of the biggest future challenges. Space, already the scarcest resource in a busy city and vital to any logistics ecosystem, will

[1]   Urbanization Trend Deck, gov.co.uk

[2]   BBC News

need to be used innovatively to accommodate every type of demand, from public to professional. The right planning can contribute to a cleaner, more efficient city and deliver jobs across different skill sets. Sustainability plays an ever-more important role today and studies suggest that as consumer preferences shift further towards ecommerce, this can have a positive impact. Built-out logistics networks, that deliver goods from urban fulfilment centres close to consumers (rather than from facilities outside of the city), can save around 50% of transport-related greenhouse gas emissions[1]. Direct-to-home deliveries should ease congestion too, when a full delivery van can on average, replace 100 individual car trips. As service levels increase and future logistics operations become cleaner and quieter, facilities themselves will gradually become a common aspect of urban landscapes again.

Technological advances are a key driver of logistics efficiency and will radically shape how towns in the future function. Smarter more interconnected cities will enable systems, devices and equipment to communicate amongst themselves, achieving an efficiency that cannot be realized by humans and which will greatly alleviate pressures on congestion and service provision. For instance, advanced analytics and IoT-based solutions like load-pooling and dynamic rerouting can reduce emissions by 10%, unit costs by 30% and congestion by 30%.[2]

Owning a car would be obsolete in the more distant future, something simply called on when needed, reducing congestion in great urban areas further as part of a shared economy mindset. Robots will enter the workforce, increasing efficiency and propping up labour shortages in a hybrid style, human co-existence. Buildings will evolve to become fully smart, equipped with sensors to monitor functions and communicate with other devices, make autonomous decisions and be more efficient using energy. In a goods flow environment, like a warehouse, utilization will be optimized and the building itself able to collaborate with the equipment and machinery inside – meaning cities themselves could become one big network.

The future supply chain can operate on these city network grids, fully connected and able to track goods from factory to end consumer. Autonomous transportation will move people and cargo efficiently across the grid, lowering congestion on road, water, rail... hyperloop, or underground mega transport highways. In this future, inner cities and last mile logistics can even be served by drones, replacing current types of mid-range vehicles, to safely deliver goods to doorsteps.

1   Prologis
2   weforum.org – the future of the last mile ecosystem

Population dense and technology rich towns of the future will be supply chain optimized. They will be greener and more efficient thanks to innovative uses of space and smart logistics configurations. Artificial intelligence and machine learning will help interconnected real estate and infrastructure, operating autonomously on city network grids, take complex, data governed decisions – keeping modern life moving and ensuring that generations to come have a more sustainable place to live.

———————

DIRK SOSEF, vice president, research and strategy, is responsible for Prologis' research and strategy initiatives in Europe. Additionally, Mr. Sosef is responsible for analyzing current market conditions and future trends, understanding the factors that drive the (logistics) property performance, and providing research-led strategy and advice to internal and external clients. He also leads and contributes to the development of best-in-class research, demonstrating Prologis' know-how and market insight.

PROLOGIS, Inc. is the global leader in logistics real estate with a focus on high-barrier, high-growth markets. As of December 31, 2021, the company owned or had investments in, on a wholly owned basis or through co-investment ventures, properties and development projects expected to total approximately 1.0 billion square feet (93 million square meters) in 19 countries. Prologis leases modern logistics facilities to a diverse base of approximately 5,800 customers principally across two major categories: business-to-business and retail/online fulfilment.

MIKE STIFF

Stiff + Trevillion

Looking back at the impact of the first lockdown in March 2020, and despite the fear and confusion, a general mood of optimism emerged. We enjoyed the clean air, the empty roads, the plane free skies and the birdsong. There was even an enhanced sense of community spirit, we were looking out for our neighbours and thanking those who run society's systems and infrastructure. Sadly, once our freedoms were restored this collaborative, optimistic and contented mood did not last long.

But perhaps that is what "The Town of the Future" could be like, a place that is fundamentally local, traffic free, connected, clean, well-served and well maintained. Historically this is how our towns and villages used to be, it was the affordability of the private motor car followed by the advent of the digital age that disrupted those community networks. The result is the dysfunctional and disconnected urban sprawl that we see almost everywhere today.

Our challenge is clear, how do we create cleaner, greener and happier environments to live in?

Over the last thirty years the digital revolution has changed our physical environments in ways that are perhaps irreversible. More importantly it has changed the way that we think and interact, it has re-wired our brains, and that is having a fundamental effect on society. Is there any point in resisting this change? It is almost certainly too late, the fabric of the Establishment has been unpicked and the balance of power has shifted. The reach of Big Tech and the internet has focussed wealth and power into the hands of a few individuals that now wield far more influence than either church or state.

Whilst this connected age has many advantages, it has changed the very nature of our society. We now seem to live in the "age of the individual", an age where "my truth" is fact and non-negotiable. An age where history and tradition are open for reinterpretation and where the tribes we belong too are no longer defined by common interests and beliefs.

Western society has regularly been through these transitional phases, as an example let's look at the 1960s. The radical youth movements of the time seemed to threaten the very foundations of "civilised" society. The establishment was fearful that the manifestations of this movement, music, art, sexuality, feminism, dress, language, etc. would displace the moral authority of the remnants of the Edwardian world that survived two world wars. We can now see that the ideas they spawned became a "new" establishment and these in turn are being questioned and re-written in an era of identity politics and critical race theory. A new set of rules are replacing those that my generation grew up with, history is no longer linear.

If we consider our built environment, it is questionable whether it is fundamentally shaped by such changes, statues may be removed, street names changed, but the foundations remain. So what will shape The Town of the Future? The biggest challenge facing all of us is the destruction of the very environment that sustains us, and we are making a very good job of doing just that. If we don't halt, and then reverse this damage, we will not survive. It is a fact that man made carbon emissions are accelerating the degradation of our planet, the built environment is responsible for 40% of global carbon emissions, so we will have to reconsider our towns, homes and lifestyles very carefully indeed.

Science has enabled us to create this situation, and more positively it has the potential to solve it. There are solutions, nuclear power could replace fossil fuels, and hydrogen is a clean source of power, a switch to all-electric will not solve the problem on its own. Power stations still burn woodchip, and batteries are an interim solution, the mining of rare earth metals used in their manufacture are part of the big problem. The solutions will inevitably change the way we live forever, it will reshape our cities, towns, villages and homes.

As the built environment changes, our dependency on data and technology will become firmly embedded in everything we do. It will help us to use less energy, to reduce the need for travel, and shops, schools, universities and office buildings will be redundant. Hospitals will become robotic. Art galleries and concert halls will be digitised, we won't need to be there to enjoy a "live" performance. In time we will self-medicate, self-educate, and we will no longer have to step beyond the boundaries of our homes to experience life.

The city, town and village as we know it, will be no more.

————————————

MIKE STIFF BA Hons, Dip Arch, ARB, RIBA, FRSA formed Stiff + Trevillion with Andy Trevillion in the early 1980s, later running the Studio's Berlin office. Over the years he has taught at Westminster, Brighton and Sheffield Universities, he regularly assesses design awards, and contributes to magazines and building reviews. He works primarily on central London commercial projects and has an overview of design across the studio.

Mike is a member of the Hounslow and Southwark Design Review panels, a BEE (Built Environment Expert) for Design Council Cabe, a Trustee of the Temple Bar Trust, Chair of Octavia Housing's New Homes Quality panel as well as being Chair of The Architecture Club.

Stiff + Trevillion

STIFF+TREVILLION are a well-established West London practice with a strong reputation for elegant and sophisticated architecture. Established in the early 1980's the studio employs around 60 people with collaboration forming the cornerstone of the practice ethos. From the development of the brief with the client, to the delivery of the project with the design team, we work as a team.

As well as architects and technicians, we employ interior and furniture designers, and this blend of skills reflects the work we do across the commercial, restaurant & retail and private residential sectors.

WELLS FARGO

The Town of the Future will probably not look the way we think it will.

We can do our best to speculate about changes in lifestyle, land use, architecture and all the other elements that go into making our urban areas – but we can be assured that there will be aspects of our predictions that make future generations laugh in the way we did when we realised that 2015 had come and gone without Marty McFly's hoverboards and flying cars.

The value of trying to predict the future of our towns does not lie in whether we get it right, neither is it just an exercise in intellectual curiosity. Its value lies in the *present*. Considering our predictions for the future gives us invaluable insight into where we want to go - and where we don't. Simply by spending time with the question, we are taking the first step towards creating our future.

The question is then, where do we want our towns to go? What is important to us?

In the UK, shifts in spending patterns, employment and lifestyle have put towns under pressure. The old model has become increasingly difficult to maintain, particularly in areas where changes in employment have had significant effect. There are much wider political and ideological questions than can be addressed here – in particular, around whether and how towns might be sustained, and around the levelling-up of regional disparities.

Assuming, however, that we have crossed that bridge, we might frame our thoughts on The Town of the Future around three themes. The first two, **efficiency** and **community**, have been the driving force for the growth of towns for hundreds of years, and these themes will continue to be key. They are the reasons we *have* towns, as well as factors in how we manage them. The third, **sustainability**, is a new focus and is another facet of how we manage those towns in the context of a world experiencing the pressures of climate change, over-population and resource constraint.

How these three themes find expression in future is likely, however, to look very different than it has in the past.

Efficiency is one of the main reasons people began to live in towns – to make the sharing of resources and communication easier. Whilst communication has been transformed in the 21st century, the need for efficient supply and delivery of resources (increasingly outside traditional retail) is still key. We can expect that need to continue to drive the growth of urban areas and for efficiency to be one of the three themes we consider in managing those areas. Efficiency goes to (i) how we ensure supply and delivery of goods and services (ii) how we use available space and resources and (iii) how we manage the town itself. We can expect to see wide-ranging changes in areas such as traffic and transport management, supply chain management, security, logistics and e-commerce, architecture and land use for better use of space, automation, waste management and local government.

Community is a second reason for the existence of towns. We may not need towns for communication in the way we did before the advent of the internet, but the human need for community has not changed. Humans are story-telling creatures – it is how we derive our internal and external identities – and community and culture have been part of our survival since our earliest days. We might expect The Town of the Future to prioritise health, housing, the arts and education in new ways, reflecting a renewed value placed on the mental and physical wellbeing of residents. This might include better and more diverse access to education, social offerings and civic interaction through cultural, educational and sports and leisure hubs, as well as new thinking around residential spaces.

Sustainability is not something our ancestors – or even recent relatives – had to consider on anything like the scale we must today. If we are to live successfully on an overcrowded planet, sustainability must be at the forefront of how we manage every aspect of our urban areas. We might expect considerations of sustainability to result in smarter, greener, buildings and infrastructure as well as public spaces. Considerations of sustainability will impact not only the design and layout (or retrofit) of towns and the buildings in them, but the ways in which they are used. Towns need to be sustainable not only in terms of climate change and use of resources, but also in terms of public health and lifestyle (as we have seen during the Covid-19 pandemic).

We might not be able to predict exactly what our towns will look like in 20, 50 or 200 years' time, but we can decide now where we hope to go, and begin to take steps towards it. Efficiency, community and sustainability must be our driving considerations as we begin to imagine new ways of living and working in a changed world.

This essay was submitted by members of the Commercial Real Estate team at WELLS FARGO, which offers specialized financing for commercial real estate developers and investors across the UK and Ireland. This essay was assembled and written by relationship managers and analysts within the loan origination and legal teams, based in London.

TOM WHITTINGTON

Savills

The towns of the future will... *have green, connected and diverse town centres at their heart that fulfil the wide ranging needs of the communities that live, work and play there.*

It is easy to be negative about the future of towns and cities, however, there are reasons to be optimistic. Town centres arguably face the greatest challenges, yet are critical to the future of our towns.

THE CHALLENGE

Many town centres suffer multiple long term voids largely because too much space is dedicated to one property use. Retail supply has outpaced growth in consumer spending, often led by demand for new larger more modern formats, out-of-town retailing and the rise of ecommerce. This has led to significant marginalisation of historic stock. By 2030, 25% (308 million sq ft) of UK retail floor space is at risk of becoming redundant.

It is only in the last century that we defined town centres as retail destinations; in reality they serve a much wider range of needs. Retail-only places rarely stack up financially and are disconnected from the communities they serve. Retail needs to be rightsized and alternative uses sought.

THE OPPORTUNITY

The 15-minute city is often cited as a solution. Instead of centralising provisions, services and facilities should be close to where people live. This reduces carbon dependency and increases community provision. The town becomes healthier and improves vibrancy, access to goods, culture and entertainment. For all its hardships, Covid provided an insight as to what life could be like if we spent more time in our communities and supported local businesses. A shift to agile working practices re-diverted spend away from city centres to local town centres and high streets.

Far from being a new phenomenon, it marks a return to an ancient and organic way of urban life, where people live, work, play, thrive and survive all within convenient proximity. Some of the world's most resilient and successful cities have evolved by defining themselves as comprising a series of linked communities. This concept can be expected to embed itself into the urban planning of many much smaller places.

This is not just about creating mixed use schemes, but creating mixed use, hybrid places. Adapting places within these principals will build resilience and community. If we continue to protect retail locations, rather than supporting only those offering the best chance of success and optimal delivery of social value to the community, the problem will persist.

These principles are in direct contrast to the urban planning paradigms that have dominated for the last century, where residential areas are separated from business, retail, industry and entertainment. Evidence suggests people are most loyal to the places they enjoy, but if they only sleep or work in a particular place there is no allegiance or relationship with the built or civic communities in which they live. While the concept relates to whole communities, the solution must start with our town centres.

There are challenges around viability of course, but increased funding opportunities can kickstart regeneration. Increasingly local authorities are gaining control of their town centre assets which enables a more holistic, pragmatic and long term view. Connecting people with goods, services, community and infrastructure has a positive impact on property values. Investment returns are aligned with growth, resilience, vitality, use which are all aligned with the people that are actively engaged in the space.

The message is: Stop protecting and start diversifying.

THE FUTURE

By transforming the way we think about our town centre we can reverse decline and build opportunity.

In future town centres will:

- Support their communities better with amenity, social and civic value, wellbeing, leisure and local businesses.
- Repurpose redundant space to more diversified uses, with greater diversification of people living and working in them.
- Create cross-pollination and synergy, where different uses feed off each other.
- Address both occupational demand and environmental concerns.
- Create sustainable transport, walking/cycling routes, community gardens and green spaces.
- See less siloed property uses that compliment rather than compete.
- Provide reliable long term investment opportunities that will help deliver increased funding.

In response, people will demonstrate their loyalty and increase footfall, which will better serve the businesses operating within them, including the retail, services and leisure offer. They will be lively, diverse, resilient, mixed use consumer hubs.

Ultimately the most resilient places will include all of these adaptations so while they may seem socially driven, there is a strong capitalist rationale too, providing investors take the long view; short term stakeholder engagement models are no longer fit for purpose.

Rethinking retail centres in this way by no means spells the end of town centres, but it may spell the end of retail centres as we know them. And that could be something to look forward to.

TOM WHITTINGTON, Director of Retail and Leisure Research at Savills, where he has advised retailers, landlords and developers for 20 years on all things retail, from store expansion strategies, shopping centre feasibility and supermarket performance. For the last 5 years Tom has been a commentator on ways of rationalising and improving retail places to address the needs created from over expansion. His passion lies with creating genuine curated mixed use spaces that serve better social value, while still fulfilling the financial expectations of investors and other key stakeholders.

SAVILLS provides multi sector consulting services and advice for commercial, residential and agricultural properties, property-related financial services and investment management. Savills operates from over 600 owned and associate offices, employing more than 39,000 people in over 70 countries throughout the Americas, Europe, Asia Pacific, Africa and the Middle East and is a constituent of the FTSE 250.

JOHN WOODMAN

Hollis

PRIORITISING PEOPLE AND PLANET

The Town of the Future will be filled with buildings that prioritise people and planet.

With the built environment accounting for around 40% of the UK's total carbon footprint, the property industry has woken up to the need to act quicker to decarbonise new and existing property stock, to reduce waste, and to ensure schemes are as sustainable as possible to mitigate the negative impacts of climate change.

This trend is only set to grow as all owners, developers, funds and occupiers look to implement sustainability programmes into their developments and existing investments. Banks and lenders have also stepped up their range of 'green finance' products, providing more loans with attractive terms to those who can show they are building sustainably.

Furthermore, a rise in sustainability measurements and standards over recent years, such as BREEAM, WELL, LEED Certification, Passive House, etc., provide the tools for building owners and occupiers to see how they are doing with meeting the sustainability criteria they have set. Government legislation, such as Minimum Energy

Efficiency Standards (MEES) and the Future Buildings Standard, are forcing the issue for those that haven't embraced this already.

Towns of the future will be full of buildings equipped with features that work to reduce energy, water and waste, and enhance the environment around them, rather than destroying it. Given that an estimated 80% of the UK's buildings that will exist in 2050 have already been built, and as many as 40% were built before 1985 when Part L of the Building Regulations (conservation of fuel and power) was introduced, most of these buildings will be ones that our industry must transform through retrofitting, rather than building from scratch.

EV charging points, secure cycle shelters and commuter facilities will be commonplace to support sustainable travel. Gas and oil heating will make way for on-site renewables, such as air or ground source heat pumps, and our skylines will be a sea of solar panels. Our lighting and ventilation will be smarter with daylight and CO_2 sensors, and our plumbing systems will save water with leak detection systems and rainwater harvesting feeds. Reusing materials as much as possible, from recycled raised access floors to carbon negative carpet tiles, will minimise waste and embodied carbon, whilst incorporating features such as 'green roofs', bird and bat boxes, and wildlife panels will encourage biodiversity and ensure buildings are enhancing the environment at every opportunity.

As well as being full of sustainable buildings, towns of the future will have people at their heart. Real estate must ensure that humans are at the centre of everything, from planning and decision making to construction and building management, and understanding how buildings are used by people and how occupiers' wellbeing can be maximised is critical to future-proofing the places we live and work.

Property that is designed around users' behaviour is quickly becoming the gold standard – for example, offices incorporating more collaborative spaces fit for hybrid working; homes equipped with separate work and living spaces; industrial properties with enough power provision to charge employees' and visitors' electric vehicles. Alongside that, maximising biophilic design features – plants, living walls, etc. – and incorporating outdoor space are becoming a priority for maximising the wellbeing of occupants, as is bringing in as much natural light as possible.

Delving deeper into the idea of humans being at the heart of future-proof real estate, the very best buildings will be ones that cater to all visitors who might ever be there, irrespective of their circumstances or abilities. That puts an obligation on building owners and advisers to create truly inclusive environments in terms of access, signage, warm welcome, facilities and interiors.

Thought needs to be given to access to all parts of a building, no matter the users' circumstances, whether visually-impaired, wheelchair-bound or autistic. From the outside – suitable parking provisions, uncluttered approaches, inviting and easily accessible entrances – to what lies within – step-free access options throughout, clear and legible wayfinding, multi-level receptions, easily accessible toilets – real estate of the future should be inclusive to all. Making these improvements will transform our experience of our towns and the buildings in them, not just for people with disabilities, but for all users and visitors.

With an ever-increasing emphasis on incorporating features that enhance the sustainability, hospitability, and accessibility of our real estate, The Town of the Future will be filled with buildings that are more useful, more inclusive, and more of an asset to people and planet than ever before.

JOHN WOODMAN is the Chairman at Hollis. Whilst he specialises in landlord and tenant work, his time these days is mainly divided between management of the business and business development. He was the first chairman of the Building Surveying Faculty of the RICS, a past chairman of the RICS Dilapidations Practice Panel, and the immediate past Master of the Worshipful Company of Chartered Surveyors.

HOLLIS

HOLLIS is a leading international, independent real estate consultancy. Established in 1991, we're now a multi-skilled team of over 450 surveyors, engineers, technical specialists, consultants, and project managers operating across the UK, Ireland, and mainland Europe.

2021/22: MEMBERS OF
THE ACADEMY OF REAL ASSETS

ALLFORD HALL MONAGHAN MORRIS

fletcher priest architects
london + köln + riga

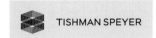

Piercy&Company

ROCKPOINT REVCAP WHITBREAD

Blackwood DERWENT LONDON CARLYLE

Ferguson Partners Schroders capital DELANCEY

Abercorn Consulting Limited   The Audley Group

Oliver Shah Limited   Tower 42 Limited   Prestbury